Fleabag and the Ring Fi

The Queen is dead. No one knows who will succeed her. Someone must find the Queen's ring within a year and a day, or the kingdom will fall.

The future looks bleak for Gemma the kitchen maid. Apart from the Queen, no one had ever shown her kindness and now the Palace Cook threatens to throw her out of the palace, back into the gutter she came from. Gemma's only friend is the mangy, streetwise cat Fleabag.

Then the Royal Fire Wielder gives Gemma a strange gift, and the courage to join the quest for the Ring. Armed with the memory of the Queen's love and urged on by Fleabag, Gemma sets out—her only guidance the memory of a voice:

'Go north by north-west...'

Beth Webb has four children and lives in Somerset. She counts storytelling and being on her own among her interests. This is her third novel for children.

To Maddy Marijke
because she likes Fleabag

Fleabag and the Ring Fire

Beth Webb

A LION BOOK

Copyright © 1995 Beth Webb

The author asserts the moral right
to be identified as the author of this work

Published by
Lion Publishing plc
Sandy Lane West, Oxford, England
ISBN 0 7459 3172 3

First edition 1995
First paperback edition 1996
10 9 8 7 6 5 4 3 2 1

Acknowledgments
My thanks to SSH for putting up with
nasturtiums and pizza.
To Capone: any similarity between the character
of Fleabag and the 'thing' that lurks up Cornhill
is purely intentional.

A catalogue record for this book is available from the
British Library

Printed and bound in Great Britain
by Cox & Wyman Ltd, Reading, Berkshire

Contents

1

Strange Fire

The tongues of flame reached higher and higher. There was no sound or smell of burning, but Gemma could feel the excitement of the growing heat against her face. There were other people there too. She did not know them, but she could see their faces dimly reflecting the orange and yellow glow.

'One day . . .' she told herself. 'One day, I shall know what it all means . . .'

Gemma shook her head and rubbed her eyes. She usually saw strange things when she looked into the depths of the great milky opal. But what she saw was different every time.

The crimson fire that glistened in the heart of the Ring's huge stone seemed still to be burning in another world, far away. Yet it was scarcely a finger's breadth from the end of her nose.

Suddenly the Queen lifted her long, thin, tired hands from the bedclothes and touched Gemma on the shoulder. 'You must not look too long into the Ring Fire, little one. You are so young . . .' Her voice trailed away. Speaking was difficult these days. The old lady was failing. Gemma could feel it in her bones, though she did not want to believe it.

The girl always brought early morning tea to the Queen. She would sit by the royal bed and wait for the old lady to waken. It was during these silent minutes she had become fascinated by the strange fire burning deep within the great Ring on the Queen's hand. The glowing flame seemed to tell her so much, yet nothing she could describe to anyone who might have asked.

Gemma made herself come back to reality. 'Shall I fetch your clothes, Ma'am? Today is the last day of the Great Festival. Perhaps you will find your successor before sunset.'

Queen Sophia raised her head and looked at Gemma with sad, grey eyes. 'And perhaps I will not,' she said slowly. 'To tell the truth, my dear, I have had enough of this festival. I have had wrestlers fighting to show how a monarch must beat all opponents, poets writing long and exceedingly boring elegies on the nature of royalty, runners bursting their lungs to exceed each other in speed to show that a sovereign must be . . . something else, I can't remember what . . .' She smiled wearily.

Gemma grinned. 'I liked the knights in armour, who wanted to kill dragons or rescue princesses to show how brave and strong they are.'

'Did you, my dear? Perhaps they did look brave and strong. Unfortunately we have no maidens in distress in our good land and we don't seem to have any marauding dragons these days. In fact we haven't had one since, oh, about a hundred years ago. I was quite a young thing in those days. It was all terribly exciting . . .

'Anyway,' the Queen added miserably, 'They're all missing the point. None of them seems to have the remotest notion of what it really means to be a king or a queen. All anyone can think about is power—all that differs is whether it is in strength or wisdom or numbers of soldiers.' She sighed. 'Fetch me today's programme, will you, please?'

Gemma was dying to ask what *was* the point. But she was a timid girl and she did not dare. Instead she got up from her stool and went to pull back the pink cotton curtains. The morning sunlight flooded the room, giving the Queen's pale cheeks a golden hue.

It wasn't at all the sort of room one would expect a queen to sleep in. It was simply furnished and always bright and airy. Gemma resolved that should she ever have a bedroom of her own, she would make it just like this one.

From the top of the desk she drew a piece of white vellum embossed with the royal crest.

'Today, Ma'am, we have jesters, more poets,' (the Queen groaned), 'some politicians,' (the Queen groaned again, even more loudly), 'a wise man and an historian. They all wish most humbly to represent to your Royal Highness their insights into what it means to be a monarch of this land . . . Oh, and there's one last entry here, in pencil at the bottom . . . your Royal Fire Welder . . .'

'The Fire Wielder,' the Queen corrected sleepily. Suddenly she opened her eyes wide. 'Is *he* coming? When?'

'It doesn't say here, Ma'am. But he's last. What does he do? Is he a fire juggler? Oh, I do hope so. I saw fire jugglers in the Great Hall last year at the

Midwinter Festival. They ate roaring flames and threw great burning torches up into the roofspace. I was sure sparks were going to get caught in the rafters, and that the whole lot would catch alight. But it didn't. It was so beautiful, I almost cried.'

'No. No. Nothing like that. The Fire Wielder is important—without him, I am no queen.' The old lady sat up and slipped her feet out from under the bedcovers. It was almost as if the last few years had suddenly been peeled away from her. 'Please help me dress, as quickly as you can.'

Gemma stared in amazement. The ancient, frail Queen Sophia was perched like a delicate bird on the edge of the bed, quite flushed and excited.

The girl lifted a sapphire-blue satin gown from the sandalwood cupboard.

The Queen shook her head and laughed. 'No, no, child, not that one. Get me my golden robes of state. I will wear my crown and my emeralds. Send for my hairdresser and my equerry and tell that pompous Prime Minister of mine to oversee the festival in my place. He will enjoy it much more than I would. Today I have more important things to attend to.'

The Queen clapped her hands in delight. 'Today is going to be a great day. Perhaps the greatest day of my entire reign!'

2

Just Look at Yourself!

The Royal Hairdresser was not hard to find and once Gemma had delivered all the other messages, there was nothing left for her to do, except to creep slowly and miserably down the back stairs to the kitchens.

Gemma had hoped to be allowed to stay and wait on the Queen for the day. She was longing to see this 'Royal Fire Wielder' who had caused Her Majesty to become so excited and alive.

But that privilege was for the daughters of lords and ladies. Gemma did not even know whose daughter she was. The Queen herself had found Gemma, a smelly, hungry ragamuffin, in the gutters of Harflorum and taken her back to the palace in the royal carriage. And as Cook reminded Gemma frequently, the gutter was where the likes of her belonged.

Cook was a fat, greasy-skinned, mean-eyed man who would always reinforce his comments on every subject with the back of a wooden spoon slammed hard on the nearest table. If it was a bad day, he would use the spoon on any of the kitchen servants who happened to be within reach.

Gemma knew today was likely to be such a day.

Cook hated festivals. They always meant extra work. This made him drink too much. Then he would get a headache. Headaches meant that everything anyone did would be wrong. And as this festival had lasted for three days, Cook's headache would be very bad by now.

The staircase down to the kitchen was not a long one. Gemma shivered. The warm glow of the fire she had seen burning in the Ring had gone. It had been only a dream. The excitement of seeing the Queen so happy was for someone else to share. Gemma descended each wooden stair one foot at a time, very slowly. Each movement brought her closer and closer to her nightmare. Two more steps and the stairs would twist to the right, bringing her to the bottom and into full view of the kitchen door.

Suddenly, she sat down hard and buried her head in her hands. She did not want to get shouted at today. She hated being beaten for nothing. Perhaps she would be better off going back to where she had come from, living off market scraps and sheltering in doorways. This was no life for anyone.

Just then a warm softness twisted around her legs. Absent-mindedly, she put her hand down and scratched the old black cat behind the ears.

'Hello, Fleabag. How are you today? I saved you some bacon rind; it's in the kitchen. When Cook goes out, I'll get it for you.'

The cat put up his ugly face and nuzzled into her hand. 'Let's go now,' he said. 'I have a little corner that needs to be filled.' He started to hobble downstairs on his three legs, but Gemma didn't move.

The cat stopped on the bottom stair and looked back at his friend. 'You don't want to go into the kitchen today, do you?' he purred in his deep, gravelly voice.

'How did you know, you old ratter, you?' Gemma laughed, scratching him under the chin with her toe.

'Dead easy,' growled the cat. 'You're sitting out here on the stairs instead of getting me my bacon rind. Don't worry, Cook is at market already. Manda and Jane have gone to help, and Harry and Tina are scrubbing out the scullery. It's quite safe.'

Gemma got up and crept stealthily into the kitchen. The great pine table had already been scoured and smelled wet and sweet. All around hung polished copper pans and ladles, moulds and shapes, bunches of herbs and baskets of eggs.

Suddenly Fleabag yowled and sprang across the room with fifteen claws unsheathed and razor sharp. The poor grey mouse that had been hiding behind the flour bin knew no more. Gemma turned her back on the scene. She knew it was most impolite to watch while the cat ate his prey.

After a few moments, Fleabag gave a small burp and a polite cough. 'Oh dear, excuse me. Um. A little chewy, but a good flavour. I must confess I let them get at the flour a little bit now and then. It does add to the quality of the final meal . . . Ho, ho, get it? The final meal?'

Gemma did not wish to 'get' such an awful joke and ignored him. 'Are you still interested in that bacon rind?'

'Later, thank you,' he muttered between licks at his paws. He was always meticulously clean. 'That mouse has nicely filled the little space I did have. Perhaps later, though?' he inquired hopefully, his shaggy black head on one side. Without waiting for a reply, Fleabag resumed the examination of his fur and whiskers. Suddenly he stopped and looked up at her with his big golden eyes.

'To be honest, I'm more interested in *you* than in bacon rind.'

'What do you mean?'

'Just look at yourself!'

Gemma went over to the big mirror where servants were supposed to check their appearance before going upstairs to wait on the Queen or her guests.

She was thin, tall, with lank, fair hair pulled back into a pony tail. A few freckles spangled her long, straight nose. She was neither pretty nor plain, although she had a feeling she could look quite nice if she wore something other than the palace regulation brown gingham issued to all below-stairs staff. But then, she was grateful to be out of rags and wearing something clean and mended.

Gemma could see nothing amiss. She straightened her apron a little, shrugged and turned round to look at the cat, who by now had sprung up onto the big table.

'Oh, you wicked animal!' she laughed, picking him up. 'Cook will cut your other back leg off if he catches you up there!'

Fleabag struggled free and landed heavily on all three paws. 'Huh, I'd like to see him try. Now, come and sit down. I need to talk to you seriously for once.'

Gemma sat obediently on the settle next to the

huge open fire, and Fleabag sat opposite her, so the light from the flames caught his golden eyes. 'Now listen. You know where you came from?'

'The backstreets.'

'Quite. Do you know where you are going to?'

'No, I'd not really thought about it ... I'll stay here all my life, I suppose. I've often thought about running away and becoming a street urchin again, but I know that's silly. I can read and write now as well as do the basic kitchen work, so if Cook gets too awful I might be able to get a job somewhere else ... But to be honest, I love the Queen. I don't want to leave.'

'How long do you think you will last here when the Queen dies?'

Gemma felt a huge lump swell up in her throat. She got up and poked vigorously at the fire until sparks rose into the black heights of the chimney. At last she looked over her shoulder at Fleabag. 'Do you think she'll die soon, then?'

'Don't you? This festival is putting a tremendous strain on her. I'd be very surprised if she lives a week. Then what will happen to you? Cook hates you because you're the Queen's pet. As soon as she's dead, you'll be back on the streets ... or even worse, kept here.'

Gemma shuddered.

'What do you suggest I do?' she asked very quietly.

The cat stretched and rolled onto his back, his three legs sticking out at ridiculously odd angles. 'You could start by scratching my tummy,' he suggested. 'That always helps me think.'

Gemma knelt down next to the cat and felt the delicious roar of his purr thundering through his fire-warmed, barrel-like body.

At last he twisted round and sat up. 'That's enough, thank you. Now, tell me, what would you like to do . . . if you could do anything?'

Gemma didn't need to think. 'I'd like to stay here and serve the Queen . . . or her successor, but you don't think that's possible, do you?'

The cat shook his head vigorously and a few dozy fleas landed on the hearth-rug.

'No. But I have a few practical alternatives. First of all, and right now,' suggested the cat, 'you must make yourself scarce. I hear Cook coming through the back gate. Then you must go and answer the front door. I hear a visitor coming up the path and the butler is busy out the back polishing silver . . . Then you must wait and see what happens next.'

Just then, Cook's irritable voice roared for Jane and Manda to hurry up. Gemma jumped to her feet and ran out of the kitchen as fast as her legs would carry her.

Fleabag decided that Gemma should be given something of a head start. Deftly he tugged something out from a hiding place behind Cook's chair and then with one bound he landed in the exact centre of the kitchen table. Between the black cat's paws lay a fat, grey rat with yellow teeth. It was very dead and very ugly.

As soon as the huge bulk appeared at the kitchen doorway, Fleabag jumped down and started to rub himself around Cook's legs, purring and mewing for all he was worth to show his master the great prize, neatly laid to view.

As Fleabag had foreseen, the Cook took the cat's tail in one hand, and the rat's in the other. Then with a powerful swing, both animals were tossed right out of the kitchen door, to land in a heap in the middle of the herb garden.

Fleabag, whose tail was very tough, simply returned the rat to its hiding place. It was the same one he brought out on all special occasions to impress Cook or to annoy the butler. The rat always did the trick, although it was getting a bit smelly these days.

Fleabag then went back to the herb garden. There he blinked and twitched his tail in the sunshine, as he watched the front door opening to admit a very special visitor.

3

The Fire Wielder

The little man on the royal doorstep was completely round in every way. Round stomach, round head and, under his flame-red fez, there glinted big, brown, round eyes.

He stood quite still for a second, then with a wide, sweeping gesture, he plucked off his hat and bowed low. As he straightened he caught Gemma in his gaze, then suddenly, he opened a wide, tooth-filled grin which cracked his face into a million wrinkles and laughter lines.

'Oh, good,' he said. 'You're here.'

Gemma was so astonished, she just stood there, gawping rudely at the stranger who was left standing on the doorstep.

At that moment, Fleabag sprang over the threshold and pushed his silky fur against Gemma's legs. 'Pull yourself together!' he ordered. 'The butler is coming!' The cat hobbled along the corridor into the dark gloom of the hallway with as much dignity as his three legs could muster.

With an effort, Gemma curtseyed and tried to clear her throat. 'Welcome, Sir. Whom do you wish to see, and who may I say is calling?'

The little man cocked his head on one side and looked at Gemma with a quizzical smile. He said nothing, but held out his hand to her. In his wrinkled palm was a tiny flicker of red flame. There was neither coal nor tinder nor match in his hand—the flame just hovered there, brightly.

Gemma gasped and looked at him wide-eyed. 'The Royal Fire Welder—I mean Wielder!' She curtseyed again, even more flustered than before. She felt herself going quite pink, then she lost her balance, stumbled backwards and landed very hard right on the butler's bunion.

The butler was a tall, thin, humourless man with a sour face the shape and colour of a lemon. With one motion, he picked Gemma up by the collar of her dress and deftly deposited her well out of sight in the shadows behind the great door.

With a perfect and obsequious bow to the visitor, he coldly invited the little man into the library to await Her Majesty's presence. As the butler closed the door, he managed to kick Gemma in the shins, hard and spitefully. He hissed: 'Get down below, and don't you ever let me catch you above stairs again. Ever! Get it?'

Gemma cowered back behind the door to wait for the visitor to pass, so she could slink off downstairs to cry alone.

But the Fire Wielder did not move. He stood dark and still, staring at the butler with a look that would have withered an oak tree. 'I wish to be attended while I wait,' he said firmly.

The butler bowed slightly. 'Of course, Sir. I will be at your disposal.'

'By that young lady behind the door.'

The butler glanced over his shoulder at Gemma's cowering figure.

'I'm sorry, Sir. You should not have been embarrassed even by the sight of her. She is a mere scullery maid and had no right to be above stairs at all. If you wish I will summon one of the ladies-in-waiting for you . . .'

The Fire Wielder stretched out one strong, brown hand and laid it firmly against the butler's chest. Then with his free hand pointing to Gemma he said clearly and slowly, 'I wish to be attended by that young lady there. I do not want a lady-in-waiting. I would like interesting conversation until Her Majesty can see me, not stuffy court pleasantries. And in the meantime I would like you, please, to go and arrange for two glasses of lemonade and a plate of Cook's best cakes to be sent up.'

Gemma wondered who this Royal Fire Wielder could be. This strange little man was obviously not the sort of person one argued with. The butler cast one deadly look at Gemma as he slid sideways out of the visitor's reach, and disappeared down the corridor.

Gemma stared hard at the floor. She dare not look up in case she giggled, although half of her wished that the Fire Wielder had not made such a fuss, because she now had yet another enemy in the palace. In his way, the butler was every bit as bad as Cook when it came to making servants' lives miserable.

Suddenly she realized that the strange little visitor was walking, or rather, waddling along the corridor ahead of her. Gemma pulled herself together and sprang to her place just behind him. As they reached the library, she opened the door wide with a flourish and a curtsey, just as she had seen the chief parlourmaid do.

At that moment there was a terrific crash from below stairs, followed immediately by Fleabag's agonized yowling and the butler's voice bellowing murderous threats at the animal. Gemma permitted herself a little grin. She could tell by Fleabag's voice that he was not really hurt, but had merely laid a successful ambush for his enemy, the butler.

The library was a bright room lined with oak bookcases and panelled walls. Tiny specks of dust floated lazily in the golden morning sunshine which streamed in from the open windows. The sweet smell of beeswax polish mingled with the scent from a bowl of roses on the table. It was a delightful place to just sit and be quiet.

The Fire Wielder sat down heavily in a big leather armchair and motioned to Gemma to pull up a stool. She hesitated. 'I'm not supposed to sit in the presence of visitors,' she said nervously.

The Fire Wielder leaned forward and smiled his big toothy grin which looked so startling against the dark golden brown of his face. 'Then let us say . . . that I am not a visitor, but a long lost friend.'

Gemma curtseyed nervously and pulled up the stool so it was opposite the little man.

He leaned back in his chair and closed his eyes as if he were very hot and tired. He pulled off his fez and ran his fingers through his grizzled, grey hair, until it stuck out at all angles. Heavy black eyebrows and a long, hooked nose gave him an air of solemnity despite his many smile lines.

After a while, when he opened his eyes, Gemma could see that they carried sadness as well as the warmth she had first noticed. At close quarters, he also seemed to be much older than she had first guessed. The Fire Wielder's heat and exhaustion were not helped by the long, heavy official robes he wore. These were made of glistening red, yellow and gold silk, stiffened and embroidered at every fold. They looked most uncomfortable, and he twitched at them miserably.

At last she realized he was peering at her from under his huge dark eyebrows. He was no longer smiling, but he still looked kind. 'Now, tell me, what is your name?'

'Gemma, sir.'

'A good name. Now, let us see if there is really any Ring Fire in this little Gem, shall we? When I opened my hand to you by the front door, what did you see?'

Gemma's mind ran wildly, trying to imagine what could be the right answer to such a question. In the end she swallowed hard and said simply, 'A tiny flame of fire, Sir. A bit like the one in the Queen's Ring . . .' She glanced up nervously. Had her answer been what he wanted to hear?

The old man nodded and smiled a little. 'Good . . .'

Just then a knock came at the door and the chief parlourmaid entered. She curtseyed and put the lemonade and cakes on a side table, giving Gemma a withering glance.

'Begging your pardon for interrupting, Sir, but Her Majesty conveys you her deepest respect and says she will be with you directly.' The woman curtseyed again and hesitated.

'That will be all, thank you,' said the Royal Fire Wielder dismissively. The parlourmaid looked as if she was bursting to know what was happening, but she could do nothing except leave. When she had shut the door and her footsteps had retreated along the corridor, the Fire Wielder turned to Gemma again.

'Now where were we? Ah yes, you saw fire, did you? Like this?' He opened his palm again—but Gemma saw nothing.

Gemma looked up, confused. 'No, Sir,' she said quietly. 'Not like that.'

'Good.' He smiled with intense satisfaction. 'Now, something to eat and drink, I think. Help yourself, you look half starved.'

Gemma felt decidedly uncomfortable. But she was hungry—and thirsty. While they ate, their mouths were too full of whipped cream and chocolate topping to talk. Gemma tried hard to think. What did she know about the Royal Fire Wielder? What had she ever learned about this strange Fire?

Nothing. Was he a sort of king, or maybe a magician? Yes, that must be it. She thought of the fire jugglers she had seen at the Midwinter Festival, and the fire eaters who performed in the market-place . . . He was not like any of them. Yet there was definitely something very mysterious about him.

And most unnerving of all, was the way he seemed almost to . . . recognize her.

The little man cut across her thoughts. 'You say you have seen my Fire before?'

Gemma coughed as some cake went down the wrong way. Her mind raced. What had she said?

He sensed her anxiety and tried to help her. 'You said my little flame was like the Fire in the Queen's Ring?'

Gemma was relieved. 'Yes, Sir. I bring Her Majesty her morning tea, and sometimes, while I wait for her to waken . . . I sit and watch her Ring . . . it's . . .' Suddenly she panicked. How could she finish what she had started to say?

'Go on,' said the Fire Wielder quietly.

Gemma took a deep breath. 'It's as if I sometimes see things in it!' she blurted out. 'There,' she thought. 'Now I'll be sacked for sure. What must he think of me?'

But instead of shouting or being angry, the strange little man simply settled back in his big armchair, laced his hands over his ample stomach and closed his eyes. 'Ah!' he murmured softly.

And that was how the Queen found the pair of them: Gemma sitting bolt upright on her little stool, staring in amazement and awe at the Fire Wielder, who, in his turn was settled in peaceful contemplation.

Suddenly Gemma became aware of the slight rustle of the Queen's silk robes and she sprang to her feet. She blushed deeply and made her best curtsey, scurrying towards the door as fast as she decently could.

The Fire Wielder opened one eye and put out a hand towards Gemma. 'No, child, don't go. Stand by my chair.' Then with great effort, the fat little man rose and stood at his full height before the Queen.

But he did not bow to his sovereign. Instead, it was the ancient Queen who slowly and stiffly knelt before the fat little man!

'My Lord Fire Wielder,' she said softly.

'Sophia, my dear lady!' he replied, offering his hand to be kissed before helping her to her feet and gathering her in a big hug.

4

Learn to Eavesdrop!

Gemma stood nervously at her post by the door. She had her instructions. If anyone knocked, she was to send them away immediately. She felt shaky and scared, but she was comforted by the soft warmth of Fleabag who had hopped in through the open window and settled himself against her feet.

The warmth of the summer morning was filled with the hum of bees and the soft murmurings of the two old friends settled in their chairs, holding hands and talking intensely. Gemma rested her head against the door-post and closed her eyes. Soon, she was drifting off to sleep.

Suddenly, she gasped. One of Fleabag's well-sharpened claws was picking at her leg. The cat was glaring at her. She bent down to push him away, but as she did so, he sprang into her arms and settled himself under her chin. Startled, she tried to put him down, but he hung on with all fifteen claws.

'Wake up, you duff-head. This involves you!'

'What?' Gemma whispered in horror.

'Eavesdrop, can't you? You really must develop the knack, you know.'

'I can't do that!' she hissed. But then she caught a glimpse of the Queen looking at her, so she whispered as quietly as she could, 'That's shocking, how could you even *think* of such a thing, you wicked cat?'

'If you're not meant to know what's happening, why do you think they told you to stay *inside* the room? If you weren't meant to hear they'd have posted you *outside*, or even better, sent you away completely. They are talking quietly so no one *else* can hear. Now wake up, you goose, and listen!' With which the impossible animal sprang to the floor and meowed to be let out.

As Gemma shut the door silently behind the cat, she caught a glimpse of the butler leaning with his ear closely pressed against the other side of the wall.

Gemma pretended she had seen nothing, but listened with satisfaction as a yowl and a crash indicated that once again the butler had fallen prey to Fleabag's tactics.

When all was quiet once more, Gemma began to listen to the conversation between the Queen and her strange visitor.

The Queen's head was bent forward as she listened to the Fire Wielder. The sun glinted on her small crown, and dazzled in the emeralds at her throat. She looked very beautiful and seemed much younger than Gemma had ever seen her. Yet the Queen was saying she felt ill and old.

'I feel in my bones that there is much evil and injustice in my kingdom, but I am too old and tired to do anything about it. I wish for nothing more than to sleep the Long Sleep and let all this slip away from me—and I have longed to talk with you, because I cannot let go until I am sure of my successor. There is no one in all my court that I can hand my Ring and my crown to. Although there are many wise and good people, none of them is the right one. I know it in my bones, and my great Ring grasps my finger with the firmness it did on the day you placed it there. It is not ready to leave me and go to another. I do not know what to do.'

And with a sinking heart, Gemma realized her beloved Queen was crying.

The Fire Wielder grasped the Queen's hand more tightly. 'I know,' he said softly. 'I have seen it. Now, tell me about this festival of yours.'

The Queen sighed. 'It was the idea of Hyrald, the Prime Minister. He thought that everyone in the kingdom should have the chance to come and say, in his or her own particular way, what it means to be the monarch. I think he hoped that the true successor would be found amongst them. It wasn't such a bad idea...'

'But it has yielded no one?' ventured the Fire Wielder.

'No one,' the Queen sighed. 'That is why I have been sending messages to you. Why did you take so long to come?' she asked sadly. 'I needed you.'

'Because I had to know what to say when I came.'

'But even your presence would have comforted me.'

The Fire Wielder smiled. 'I know. But I might have been tempted to speak words which were not yet ripe.'

'And are your words ripe now?'

The old man turned his head and looked out of the window at the rose garden and the wonderful view across the green slopes of the South. 'I will speak the words, and together we will see if they are right or not.

'Firstly, you must know that I too am tired and ready to sleep the Long Sleep. My heart is not strong, and I think that when you surrender your Ring, I will follow you quickly into the Quiet Place. I too must find a successor. So listen to what I suggest, and tell me if it sounds true Fire Speech in your ears.

'I propose that you place your Ring into my hands . . .'

Without hesitation, the Queen began to tug at the jewel, but the old man prevented her with a gentle motion. 'Not yet. Listen first. See if you agree. Tonight we will perform the rite of severance which will remove the Fire from the Ring. The flame will remain here at the palace, for all to see, and the Ring will be hidden where only a king or a queen would ever dare to look for it.'

'Can the Fire survive without the Ring?' The Queen sounded worried.

'As you know, my dear Sophia, the Fire is not from this world. It will quickly fade if it does not have a place where it is welcome to dwell. I believe that if I hold the Fire, it will burn for a time without the Ring—but my strength can hold it no longer than a year and a day.

'In that time, your subjects high- and low-born, young and old may search for the Ring, and whoever finds it and brings it here may prove to be the new ruler of our land. If the wrong person finds it by accident, or if a rogue or villain takes it by force, the Fire will not acknowledge him or her.

'Thus all your subjects may see and know openly that if the Fire welcomes the Ringholder, that the person will be the chosen one. If the Fire burns the holder or fades in his or her hand, that person is a usurper and not to be acknowledged.'

Both were silent for a very long time.

At last Queen Sophia said, 'It is a terrible risk, my Lord.'

The Fire Wielder leaned forward and looked earnestly into the Queen's eyes. 'But is it a wise risk, my Lady? Is it the *right* one?'

The Queen eased her tired back into the chair's depths, and closed her eyes. At last she spoke. 'If, when the moment comes to perform the rite of severance, the Fire burns bright and clear, let us proceed. If it fades and seems sickly, let us wait and see what else may befall.'

With a sigh the old man smiled. 'Such were my thoughts, your Majesty.'

Just then, Fleabag once more reappeared on the window-sill. He stretched his untidy, black shape into a long shadow which fell across the Queen's lap. She looked up and laughed, patting the chair arm beside her. 'Don't you dare sit on my best frock, you old Fleabag, you,' she said playfully. 'I suppose you have been listening, you wicked animal?'

Fleabag said nothing as he sprang up next to his mistress, but purred delightedly as she scratched behind his ear.

'Now, listen, you old rogue. I have an important job for you.' Fleabag stopped purring and sat to attention, staring at the Queen with wide, golden eyes. 'I know you understand every word I say and I'm sure you repeat most of it to your equally disreputable cronies below stairs. But this is a secret. I want you to look after Gemma over there. She will have a difficult time ahead, and two heads are better than one, even if one is filled with furry nonsense and fish scraps. Will you take on the care of a mere human, old friend?'

Fleabag did not answer, but jumped down and strode across the room until he reached Gemma's feet. There he sat and looked at her until she picked him up. But there were no claws this time. Just velvet paws and a deep, rich, rolling purr.

Gemma looked at the Queen in astonishment. What could she mean?

The Fire Wielder beckoned the girl over. 'Give me your hand,' he said. He laid his palm across hers and, when he took it away again, Gemma jumped, for there, burning brightly in the hollow of her hand, was a tiny flicker of flame.

There was a strange burning in her palms. But it made her feel indescribably happy.

Suddenly it was gone, and she felt quite lost and alone. 'Remember that little flame, whatever happens,' he said quietly. 'Now, go and call Her Majesty's Equerry and the Prime Minister. We have much to do before nightfall.'

5

The Ring and the Fire

'Just do as you're told, will you?' The cat looked most irritable. 'We have a lot to do before nightfall too.'

'But I've got work to do. I'm supposed to be in the kitchens. They'll miss me.'

'Let them miss you!' growled the cat, jumping up onto Gemma's bed. 'You're not going back there again. Now get on and start packing, will you? Not much, just the essentials. You don't want to be slowed down by *stuff*. Mind you,' he muttered, 'I don't see why humans need luggage anyway. Look at us cats—we're always immaculately dressed for every occasion, and we never carry anything.' Fleabag struck what he hoped was an artistic pose.

'Were you travelling light when you forgot to pack your fourth leg?' teased Gemma.

The cat bristled his long black fur in disgust and turned his back. 'You're avoiding the real issue,' he said haughtily. 'We've no time for banter. Get packing, will you?'

'But where are we going?' asked Gemma. 'How will I know what to do next?'

'Oh, do stop pestering me with stupid questions,' moaned Fleabag. 'You'll find everything out in good time. But above all, make sure you're in the Throne Room at sunset. There's going to be a proclamation. Get there early, for the rest of the world will be there as well.

'Now leave me in peace, do. I need my sleep. You don't know what a hard life it is, being a cat.' And with that, the incorrigible animal curled up on his favourite cushion at the end of Gemma's bed, and went to sleep.

Gemma looked at him in exasperation. But what could she do? Once Fleabag was asleep, an earthquake would not shift him until he was quite ready to waken. In the end she shrugged and looked around. The attic bedroom was shared by all six of the youngest maids and a very little boy who blackened boots. Every child had a small cupboard for personal possessions and clothes. When she had arrived at the palace Gemma had had nothing but what she was wearing, and that was quickly burned. In its place she had been given two gingham kitchenmaid's dresses and someone's cast-off red skirt and white blouse for holidays.

Well, Fleabag wasn't intending to allow her to work here again—for a while at least—so she changed into her holiday things. Her underclothes and hairbrush she wrapped up into a bundle with her old grey cloak.

Just as she was tying a knot to secure it all, she heard her name being yelled by the under-chambermaid in a furious temper.

When she saw Gemma out of uniform, she

screeched even more loudly and, without giving Gemma a chance to say a word, pushed her out of the door and down the stairs. In between the woman's tirade—how she had exhausted herself looking for the good-for-nothing guttersnipe all over the palace—Gemma gathered that the Queen was calling for her.

Standing outside the door of the royal bed-chamber, Gemma breathed deeply and tried to collect her wits for a few seconds. At last she knocked and went in.

The Queen was sitting alone in the room. Her jewels were put away and her long grey hair was spread loose over her thin shoulders. She had been crying, for her eyes were damp and slightly red. But she looked calm and even happy in a strange way.

Gemma curtseyed and apologized for being late. The Queen shook her head and smiled. 'Please don't worry. There will be time for everything, I am sure. Now please help me change. I won't need these robes of state any more. I will wear my white linen gown and the green shawl.'

Gemma unfastened the Queen's robes and helped the old lady step free from the encum-brance of their folds. The linen dress was quite plain and light, and the warm pale green shawl was soft and comforting. Gemma brushed the old lady's hair and gathered it into a pink ribbon.

Suddenly the Queen looked no longer like Her Majesty. She was a granny—a friendly, loving, very old granny.

Impulsively Gemma sobbed and cuddled her. How she had always wished for a granny of her own. The Queen stroked the girl's hair and rocked her. After a little while she pushed Gemma gently away. Her eyes were damp again. Perhaps she had always wanted a granddaughter like Gemma.

'My dear, we will not talk again. Not this side of the Long Sleep. I want you to sit still and listen very carefully.' Gemma sat obediently on the little stool and took the Queen's hands in her own.

'Now, you heard my Lord the Fire Wielder and me making our plans this morning? Good. I want you to join this quest.'

Gemma looked up in surprise. '*Me*, your Majesty? You know I would do anything within my power for you, but what use can I be?'

The Queen looked serious. 'Listen. You have studied my Ring more than any of my subjects. Have you ever wondered why I picked *you* up from the street when there are so many urchins who need homes?'

Gemma shook her head. She had never understood why she had been chosen.

'It was because I saw you looking into my Ring as I passed. Not *at* it, as everyone else does, you understand, but *into* it. I knew we would need each other one day. Since then I have often watched you looking into the depths of the stone while you thought I slept.

'You of all people will recognize the true stone in whatever guise you may see it. You may be needed to protect it from an evil person taking it by force, or to prevent a forgery being foisted on my people.

'You alone can do this, Gemma. Will you do it . . . for me?'

Gemma swallowed hard. Suddenly she felt very small and particularly useless. 'Ma'am, I ... I'm sure ... but for you, since you ask it, yes, I will.'

The Queen smiled and nodded, patting Gemma's hand absent-mindedly. 'Yes, Gemma, do it for me. And look after my cat Fleabag, will you? He lost his leg in a great act of heroism and he holds a noble title and a great name. But it is more than my life is worth to tell you, so never let on you know ... And,' at this the Queen leaned over conspiratorially to whisper in Gemma's ear, 'you probably won't believe this ... but Fleabag is a *talking* cat!'

'Yes, Ma'am,' Gemma replied, trying not to giggle.

The Queen straightened herself and sighed. 'I would very much like to give you a parting gift, but I fear that if anyone saw you with a jewel of mine they would not believe I had given it and would imprison you for theft.' Then she smiled. 'Take my shawl, child. Your clothes are hardly fit for the journey you must make. And your feet are almost the same size as mine, so take my good walking shoes from my cupboard. Just fetch me another shawl, please. It doesn't much matter what I wear now. My part is over.'

Gemma swallowed hard to try to rid her throat of the great lump that stuck in it. She wrapped a delicate pink shawl around the Queen's old shoulders. Then she dressed herself in the Queen's gifts.

Leaning on Gemma's arm, the old lady rose rather shakily to her feet.

'Now take me into the Hall of Light where the Royal Fire Wielder awaits me. There we will say goodbye.'

Gemma could not speak. She obeyed silently. The Queen seemed to have aged immeasurably since that morning. As they walked slowly down the long, dark corridors, Gemma held the Queen's arm firmly. The old lady moved more and more slowly with every step as age and tiredness seemed to descend upon her.

At the final turn, Gemma glimpsed Fleabag, watching his mistress open the door to the Hall of Light for the last time. He stepped out and rubbed his fur against the Queen's legs and she bent down and scratched behind his ragged ear. He purred and licked her hand, then she stood up straight, and entered the Hall.

'Go and get your bundle and meet me in the Throne Room. It's almost time. Hurry!' hissed the cat.

Gemma did as she was told. Strangely, no one seemed to notice or even recognize her as she slipped between the palace staff. They were too busy arranging chairs for the invited nobility and bringing up trays of refreshments for the guests.

Soon Gemma and Fleabag had possession of a small corner behind a pillar, where they would be able to hear and see what went on without being seen themselves.

'I almost didn't recognize you,' mewed Fleabag. 'You look posh in that outfit.' Gemma looked down. Of course, in her holiday skirt and the Queen's shawl, she looked quite different. That must be why she had slipped through unnoticed. She smiled and stroked the cat's ears.

'What's going to happen?' she whispered.

'Sssh! You'll see,' he hissed.

The room was quickly filled with throngs of all the nobility, royal advisers, courtiers and, of course, the knights who formed the Queen's Guard. Low voices buzzed with discreet concern and subdued excitement. Rumour had spread fast that this was going to be a momentous occasion. Everyone was dressed in glittering robes; the room was aglow with dazzling silks and satins, mingled with the gleam of polished dress swords and gold embroidery.

Gemma shifted to try to ease the cramp that was creeping up her leg. She would have loved to join the crowd, but she knew she would stand out like a sore thumb in such a company.

Just then a trumpet fanfare greeted the arrival of the Royal Fire Wielder, comfortable at last in a white linen shirt and loose white trousers. The Queen was carried in on a sedan. She was too weak to rise, but she greeted the people with a lift of her hand.

The Royal Fire Wielder stepped forward and addressed the crowd.

'My Lords and Ladies,' he bowed to left and right. 'Today, the Queen Sophia has surrendered the Ring of the Kingdom and now she goes to sleep the Long Sleep in the Quiet Place. I too will join her soon, but our successors have not yet been found. To this end, today, in the Hall of Light, I performed the rite of severance.

'This Ring,' he announced, holding the jewel high for every one to see, 'is now quite simply an opal ring . . .' He paused, then he added, 'And the Fire resides with me.' At this point he opened his other hand and held his arm up high. Everyone in the Throne Room gasped, for from his palm leapt a great tongue of fire which blazed as high as the gold and white domed ceiling, casting its dazzling light all around.

Gemma clutched at Fleabag so hard he yowled. She could not describe her feelings—a tangle of joy, recognition and fear. But then the light was gone again, just as quickly. The Fire Wielder had closed his hand.

'The Ring will be sent by secret messengers to a place where only the true successor to our great Queen will dare to find it. The Fire I will hold here, in the Hall of Light, until the Ring is found and returned.

'When the two are truly reunited, the next queen or king will be known. Tomorrow, all those who will, be they noble, servant or farmer, may commence the search. If the Fire and the Ring are not brought together within a year and a day, the Fire will fade and slip back to the Other Place from whence it came and we will be left blind and lost.'

At this, the Royal Fire Wielder turned and walked out of the room, followed by the Queen and her bearers.

Silence hung heavily as the listeners sat stunned by what they had heard. At last, in twos and threes, the people began to drift away from the Throne Room.

Everyone was so shocked, the supper had barely been touched when the last visitors had gone. The girl and the cat stayed hidden in their corner until the room was empty. Then Fleabag gave Gemma a soft nibble. 'Time to move. But first things first: food.'

To Gemma's horror the cat jumped up onto the table and began to eat his fill. 'Come on,' he muttered through a mouthful of fishpaste sandwiches. 'This is good. Fill up and take some for tomorrow. You don't know when you may eat again.'

Gemma saw the point. She filled her pockets with dried fruit, and pushed hunks of bread and cheese into the end of her bundle. Just as she began to eat, a footman caught sight of them and chased them out of the Throne Room. With a flick of his tail, Fleabag leapt to the floor and sprang ahead down the corridor with something large and heavy in his teeth.

At last they reached the little back stairs behind the kitchen where they had often sat and talked. No one was about. A few more steps brought them to the boot cupboard where they could eat in peace. As they went in, Fleabag presented Gemma with his loot . . . a whole chicken! 'Waste not, want not,' grinned the cat. 'Wings or breast?'

scared. It's just that it's something *you* have to do. Not me.'

Gemma put her tired head against the door. The coolness of the wood calmed her racing brain. 'You're right,' she said at last. 'I've got to talk to him.' Then, with a small but determined push, she opened the little door that led into the Hall of Light.

The circular room was quite silent and almost dark. Its walls were plain white stone with tall, thin lancet windows set high and close together, forming a huge glass lantern in the ceiling above. Everywhere grey and purple shadows mingled with the soft, gentle light of the early evening stars shining in the indigo sky. The thin, white crescent moon was just rising over the lowest window-ledge. The quiet and calm of the room invited Gemma to sit on the floor, where she stayed quite still until her eyes adjusted to the gloom.

As she looked around the room, Gemma noticed a tiny, flickering light in the very centre. She stood up quietly and stepped forward. 'Fire Wielder?' she whispered. 'Is that you?'

There was no answer. She called again. Although there was no reply, the silence seemed to be full and alive; it did not feel like an empty room.

She stepped gingerly toward the flame. It seemed to be very close. She reached out her hand towards it and called again.

There was still no answer, but this time she added, 'Fire Wielder, if you're here, help me please. I don't know where to go, or what to do next. In all the world I've only got Fleabag, the cat. Do you remember him? Oh I wish you were here. Perhaps you could come with us to find the Queen's Ring and we could give it to the right people.'

She was silent. A round, dark shape dissociated itself from the rest of the shadows as the Fire Wielder moved forward. As he reached the little table where the flame burned, his kind, wise face suddenly appeared, lit by the tiny gleam of golden light.

'My little Gem,' he said with a smile in his voice. 'I'm sorry I did not hear you. I was asleep.'

Suddenly Gemma wished she hadn't come. She felt silly. She wanted to run and find Fleabag and disappear into the night—to go back to the little street behind the market where she used to live. What business did a street urchin have here?

She turned to run, but the Fire Wielder's firm hand prevented her. 'Whatever you have need to know, ask, child. But don't ask me. Look steadily into the flame, and be sure the Fire Giver will answer you.'

Gemma did not notice when the Fire Wielder let her go. She was transfixed by the flame. She could not move. The light did not hurt her eyes, but once again, it made her intensely happy and terribly sad all at once.

After what seemed an age she whispered, 'Where do I go now? What do I do?'

Gemma never knew whether she heard the voice with her ears, or simply 'knew' the answer. But she knew it for certain. The Ring Fire had told her to go north by north-west.

She was so astounded she screamed and ran. Like a terrified fieldmouse caught in one of Fleabag's traps, she darted in panic-stricken terror from one side of the strange room to the other. At last she glimpsed the door opening slowly as the big brass handle caught the light of the almost fully risen moon. With one last effort, she bolted for the gap, only to collide with a very solid and firmly built figure which barred her way.

Strong hands caught Gemma under the arms and swung her round to face the centre of the room. Gemma felt the cold weight of chain mail against her face and leather gauntlets against her skin. The grip was one of iron and there was no resisting.

'What shall I do with this intruder, my Lord?' came a deep voice. 'Shall she be horsewhipped?'

'Certainly not!' came the Fire Wielder's indignant reply. 'Take the child to an inn. Feed her, give her a good night's sleep and in the morning listen to her story. She has much that will be useful to you. Remember that even guttersnipes are important in the eyes of the Fire Giver. And remember above all that you are sworn to defend *all* the Queen's people, whether high- or low-born, and whether washed or unwashed. Even kings and queens may come disguised in rags to see how their servants treat the lowliest of their subjects.'

'As you wish, my Lord.'

The Fire Wielder spoke again. 'My Lady Knight Rowanne de Montiland, I give you Gemma Streetchild. Gemma, I give you the Lady Rowanne. Now I must sleep again, for I am weary.'

And with that the dark, round figure lay back on his couch which was now visible in the strengthening starlight.

Outside the door, in the light of the torches which had now been lit, Gemma twisted in the unyielding grasp to try to get a look at whoever was holding her. All that was visible was a tall, muscular figure clad in leather and closely-wrought chain mail. Over the mail shirt was a silk-embroidered tabard showing the arms of one of the Queen's Guard. A small, pointed helmet cast deep shadows across the wearer's face.

'Just let me get my bundle,' Gemma begged and the figure grunted, loosening her hold.

As they reached the gates the duty soldier saluted the mail-clad captor, but barred Gemma's way.

'What are you doing at this entrance, girl? The servants' door is at the back. Surely you know that!'

Gemma spoke quickly. 'I'm on an errand. I'm sent out with an urgent message.'

'Don't give me none of your lies! Brat!' and the man swung his arm as if to deliver Gemma a box on the ear.

With a swift hand Gemma's captor caught the man's wrist. 'It is a very important and secret message, Gordik. I am escorting her to make sure she comes to no harm.'

The sentry guard shook his arm free of the grasp and grunted, 'Funny messenger.'

'The ways of the Fire Wielder are mysterious and not to be questioned,' uttered Gemma's guard with authority.

Gordik shrugged and grunted. 'That's as may be. If she wasn't with you, my Lady, I'd send her to the sergeant. Goodnight.' And the man strode back to his brazier, where he very determinedly looked away as the two left the palace precincts and turned down an alley to the left.

A few minutes later a third shadow left the palace, running with a strange hopping motion. The three-legged cat ignored Gordik's offer of a bit of meat, as Fleabag, too, left the comfort of his home for the dark of the city night.

7

The Queen's Cat

In the oak-panelled comfort of the inn the Lady Knight Rowanne de Montiland removed her corselet of mail. Gemma stared in amazement. Even without her armour, her Ladyship could never pass as an ordinary woman. Her long dark hair was coiled at the nape of her neck, and a fine, well shaped face showed annoyance and distaste. Her eyes and her whole demeanour were haughty; she made it quite clear that she had no intention of having anything to do with Gemma once dawn had broken. She would obey the Fire Wielder to the letter, but that was all.

Fleabag sat under the table and settled himself comfortingly around Gemma's feet. He had his eyes closed, but he was listening to every word.

'Well?' the knight demanded. 'What have you to tell me, guttersnipe?'

Gemma sipped from the pot of ginger ale she had been given. The bread and meat looked appetizing but, after sharing a whole chicken with Fleabag, she was not very hungry. Anyway, she was too tired to eat. When the knight wasn't looking she would slip the food into her bundle for tomorrow.

'I'm waiting!'

Gemma looked at Rowanne de Montiland. Was she her saviour or her captor? 'What do you want to know, my Lady?'

'Whatever you have to tell. The Most Noble Fire Wielder told me you have important information for me. Why else do you think I have wasted good money on your bed and food? Now tell me quickly before I return you to Gordik and his friends.' The knight pushed her beer aside and sprawled forward on her elbows, until her glowering features were only inches from Gemma's face.

Gemma leaned as far back as she dared without falling off her stool.

'I . . . I really don't know what I must tell you, my Lady. If I knew, I would tell you without hesitation. You have indeed been most kind . . .'

At that moment, Fleabag crept out from under the table and sat down right in front of Lady Rowanne's nose.

With a most unknightly squeal Rowanne knocked her beer flying and sprang back three paces. As she leapt she grabbed her stool with one hand and drew her sword with the other.

'Cats!' she screamed. 'Someone's let a cat in here!'

Fleabag bristled his tail like a bottle-brush. 'Snobs!' he squealed. 'Someone's let a snob in here!'

This made the knight scream all the more loudly, bringing three of the most burly men in the bar to her rescue, which did not please her at all.

Gemma was reduced to a heap of helpless laughter on her stool. Matters were made worse when the men, who thought they were rescuing a fair damsel from the grasp of terrible villains, realized what was happening and also began to laugh fit to burst.

Rowanne grew redder and redder until she could stand the embarrassment no longer. She rapidly hid her Queen's Guard tabard under Gemma's bundle so no one could guess her real rank, then she packed the girl off to their room. Ahead of them, like a royal equerry, strode the black shadow of the noble Fleabag. His head was high, his tail erect and his stride strong and brave.

At the bedroom door, Rowanne reached ahead and pointed the naked blade of her sword at the threshold. 'Come one paw stride nearer, puss, and by all I hold precious, I will have your fur for a collar.'

'No, you won't,' said Fleabag coolly. 'I've got fleas.'

The knight caught the pommel of her sword into a firmer grip as the blade touched the cat under his chin, bringing his head round so that they both glared at each other. His golden eyes met her dangerous, bright blue scowl. Neither blinked.

'Cat,' she said icily at last, 'I dislike cats of any description ... unless they are fighting Toms, on whom I might have a bet. I concede such a bet won me the velvet cloak I wear ... But unless you are such an animal,' here she ran the sharp blade along Fleabag's back, 'which, after consideration, I doubt ... then fleas or no, I will have you dead at my feet unless you remove yourself NOW.'

At that moment she took a lunge at Fleabag. The cat guessed her move and twisted round so that her sword pierced only the air where his fourth leg should have been.

'Missed!' he sang gleefully. Then with one bound he leapt onto a high beam which supported the door frame. From there he could survey his new found enemy more clearly. 'Guess what?' he spat, 'I don't like snobs much either. Not even fighting snobs. And what's more,' he sneered, 'I grew my own cloak. I didn't have to win it with a wager.

'Now,' he hissed, 'are we going to bed or what? We have a long day ahead tomorrow and I am quite exhausted!'

The Lady Rowanne turned with disdain to Gemma. 'Take this ... creature out to the back yard, child!'

Gemma shook her head, suppressing a grin. 'I'm sorry, my Lady, but I can't do that. He was the Queen's cat, and I'm not sure whether he was given to me as *my* pet, or if I was given to him as *his* pet ... but it appears we are together.'

Fleabag preened his fur and looked smug.

Even in the dim torchlight it was easy to see that the Lady Knight Rowanne de Montiland was quite puce with rage. She spoke very slowly. 'If that ... cat so much as enters that room, I sleep here on the doorstep.'

Fleabag landed gracefully on the ground in front of his adversary and pushed at the door with both forepaws. 'Fair enough,' he said. 'Suits me.' And he marched inside.

8

The Paladin

Rowanne de Montiland did not sleep well. Military training had, of course, prepared her to bivouac under all conditions, but it was her fury at being defeated by a mere cat which kept her awake all night. Now, at last, dawn was breaking and its grey light was seeping under the thatch outside the window.

Rowanne got up stiffly from the corridor floor and eased her protesting muscles until she was more or less upright. Gingerly, she creaked the bedroom door open. That wretched animal was curled up and fast asleep on the girl's bed. She looked at the second, unslept-in bed. It was so inviting. She glanced at the cat. Not a whisker moved. If she just lay down on the bed for a few minutes she could close her eyes and ease her aching back a little . . .

When she woke it was almost mid-morning. The golden sun was streaming in at the window with May warmth. Gemma was leaning over her with a tray of bread and honey and a tankard of fresh, foaming milk.

The Lady Rowanne flung back the covers in a

rage. How could she actually have *slept?* She was meticulously disciplined and could wake or sleep as needed.

She grudged thanks at Gemma and took the tray. Before she ate, she tentatively glanced around the room, but the dreaded cat wasn't there. At least she could eat in peace. As she tore at the bread with strong white teeth, she absently watched Gemma tidying the room and remaking her own bed with fresh sheets. It wasn't her job, but she did it well and quickly.

Gemma finished the work, stood before the knight and curtseyed. 'I thank you for your care, my Lady. I would gladly tell you what you wish to know, but as I don't know what it is I cannot help you. Now I must be on my way, as I do in truth have an urgent task to perform for Her Majesty. If I can be of any further service to you before I leave, pray tell me, so I can perform it speedily.'

Rowanne spread some more thick, yellow honey on her bread. 'Where are you going?'

'North by north-west.' Gemma replied promptly as she picked up her bundle and sat on the made bed. 'Do you by any chance know where that is?'

Rowanne licked the dripping honey from her fingers. 'Yes. Go through the Beggar's Gate and keep on that road. But why are you in such a hurry to see what lies north by north-west? There's not much to interest a child along there. No fairs or entertainments for many long miles.'

Gemma hesitated and fiddled with the corner of her bundle. She pulled her mouth into a small, pink shape and thought silently for a few seconds. At last she decided that it did not matter if this strange woman laughed at her. She would never see her again, anyway. She looked up and kept her large, green eyes steady on Rowanne's face.

'The Ring Fire told me to go that way.'

'Don't be silly, child,' scoffed the knight as she took a long drink of milk.

Gemma flushed deeply and stood up. She pulled herself to her full height and stuck out her small, sharp chin. Looking down at the Lady Rowanne, she stammered, 'I may be only a child to you, but to Her Majesty, I was someone fit to send on an errand. And I will do it until I succeed or die. So there!' And with that she stamped her foot and ran for the door.

Rowanne sniggered into her bread as she took another bite. But she did not enjoy her food. Fleabag had suddenly appeared on the table right in front of his new enemy.

'That was ill done, Ma'am,' he commented with gravity.

Rowanne did not scream this time. She merely picked the cat up by the scruff of his neck and went to the window. It was quite a long drop onto cobblestones below.

The cat merely twisted in Rowanne's grasp and sunk his claws so deeply into her skin she could not shake him off. As she bit her lip in pain and struggled in vain to release herself from his grasp, the cat spat at her:

'Fool! You asked to know the important message Gemma had to tell, and you laugh when you are told it. You are not fit to be a paladin on this quest.'

Rowanne balked at the cat's words and gingerly pulled him back over the window-sill, dumping him on the nearest bed. His fur was standing on end and his great eyes glowed like watchmen's lamps. 'What did you say?' she gasped as she nursed the torn skin on her hands.

Gemma stepped back into the room and picked up Fleabag tenderly. 'He said, I told you what you wanted to know, though I don't know what that can have been, and you're not fit to be a . . . a something on this quest.'

Rowanne spoke coldly and precisely. 'A paladin— a knightly companion—on what quest? The one to find the Queen's Ring, you mean?'

'I don't know what anyone means,' replied Gemma unhappily. 'I just know the Queen told me to join in the quest. She said that I of all people would recognize her Ring when it's found. And it is my responsibility to make sure that no frauds are passed off as the real thing. That was the Queen's command and when I asked the Fire Wielder where I should start, he said ask the Ring Fire. So I did, and that's what I was told. North by north-west.' Gemma paused to catch her breath. She was not used to long speeches, especially in front of daunting people like this knight.

Rowanne sat down hard on a stool and leaned her head on her hands. Her long black hair was loose and her face was white. She looked almost ill. 'The Ring Fire really spoke to you?' she asked very quietly.

Gemma shrugged. 'I don't know, my Lady. I can't answer that. I'm just trying to do what the Queen asked me to do because I love her and I'd do anything for her. But it's so worrying and confusing that at the moment I wish it would all just go away!'

The girl spoke with such a firm conviction that Rowanne could not help but believe her. She sat quite still, then with a suddenness that made Gemma jump, the knight stood up and thumped the table with her fist.

'Then let us prove that abysmal cat wrong. Let us go north by north-west together. My squire broke his leg two weeks ago and may take a long time to mend. I noticed that, for a guttersnipe, you work well. If you will come with me as my squire or maid, or whatever you choose to call yourself, I will feed you and give you my protection on your journey.'

Still hugging her bundle tightly, Gemma watched the knight warily. 'And what about Fleabag?'

'Oh, he won't want to come. Cats never travel far from home.'

'This one does.' Fleabag jumped down to the floor and surveyed Rowanne de Montiland coolly. 'And I have sworn to stay with Gemma Streetchild for as long as she may need me.'

'I also wish to stay with Fleabag,' added Gemma. 'Her Majesty told me to trust him. But,' she added, looking Rowanne hard in the eye, 'she never said the same thing about you!'

Rowanne was furious at the insult, but she fought down her anger. If what she had heard was true, the ways of the Fire Wielder were mysterious indeed! There must be something very special about this child. And from her eyes and her whole manner, she was obviously telling the truth—every word. Although it did not make sense . . .

Yet, why shouldn't she take Gemma north by north-west? Her cousin Rupert had his palace there, and he was closely connected to the Queen's household. Perhaps the Ring had been hidden there . . . and what if she should succeed in finding it, without mentioning the purpose of her visit to dear cousin Rupert? A simple test of showing it to the child might ensure . . . great things for her own future. She would reward the girl suitably of course, a purse of gold—or maybe silver and a job as under-parlour-maid at the palace. She could see it all!

Yes, she must go on the quest herself. The Fire Wielder had hinted as much. But she must get the child on her side—and get rid of that cat . . .

At last she spoke. 'If the cat goes, I stay here.' The knight puckered her dark eyebrows and glared at her opponents.

'Fair enough,' called Gemma, as she reached the door of the room again and slipped her foot around the jamb. Then, with a dash, she and the agile cat had sprung away along the corridor.

The Lady Rowanne's heart sank. How could Gemma possibly not be honoured beyond all imagining by her offer of escort? She had to get the child back and win her confidence.

Suddenly she realized there was quite a hubbub outside. With three long strides she crossed the room and leaned out of the window. Below, crowds were gathering in the streets, and people were howling and crying as if the end of the world were nigh.

With a feeling of dread, Rowanne gathered up her few belongings and ran downstairs. She paid the innkeeper, who was far too busy peering out at the street to take any real notice of the money she handed him.

'What's going on, landlord?' she asked.

The young man blew his nose on his apron and peered at Lady Rowanne with puffy eyelids. ' 'Tis Her Majesty, my Lady. She died about a hour ago. Quiet-like in her sleep, they say. The funeral is to be next week, but now everyone is in mourning and turmoil, for 'tis said she named no successor. 'Twill be a worrying and tumultuous time ahead, by my reckoning.'

Suddenly, Rowanne was gripped with a clear-cut certainty. She must find Gemma. But a street child like that could slip away unseen in seconds. How could she ever find her in these crowds?

'Did you see which way the child and the cat went?' she persisted.

The landlord scratched his head, letting dandruff fall onto his shirt. 'Can't rightly say I did,' he said. I've been watching the crowds, you see, Ma'am. Them's in an ugly mood and I'm worried, there's the truth of it.'

Rowanne clicked her tongue in annoyance and dashed out into the street. She did not have to look far. Rushing crowds had pushed Gemma hard against the wall of the Town Hall opposite.

With effort she waded her way through the mass of people until she was close enough to shout to Gemma. At last, Rowanne managed to catch her eye.

Gemma opened her mouth in a wordless cry. The girl's face was wet with sweat and tears. She was terrified, pinned by a surging, ever-increasing press of heavy bodies, pushing and shoving their way towards the palace.

With all her strength, Rowanne kicked and elbowed her way through. Gemma was pale under her freckles and her hair was loose and dishevelled. Suddenly her eyes stared wildly and her knees buckled as she fainted. Rowanne forced her way alongside the crumpled figure, planted her legs far apart and braced her arms against the wall, making herself into a human cage protecting Gemma against the crowd.

Despite the battering of the crowds thundering along the narrow street, Rowanne de Montiland did not move. Something tickled her feet occasionally, but she did not look. She dared not even turn her head. It was only when she noticed that people sometimes shouted in pain and jumped away from them that Rowanne realized the tickle was Fleabag, squatting between her feet and scratching and biting at anyone who came too close.

Eventually the crowd lessened to a trickle. Rowanne scooped Gemma up and carried her back to their room at the inn. She paid for a second night for them both and left Gemma sleeping off her shock. Then, furnished with a tankard of good beer, she sat in the empty taproom and thought long and hard.

9

Round Two to Fleabag

Several hours later Rowanne peered around the door of the darkened bedroom. The cat was sitting bolt upright on Gemma's bed.

'Um...' ventured Rowanne, who really did not have the first idea of how to be polite to a person, let alone a cat. 'Um, Mr Cat—will you look after Gemma? Don't let her go until I get back, will you? I'm only going to get supplies, not a cage.' The cat stared coldly at the knight, but remained infuriatingly silent.

Rowanne tried again. 'Do you think she needs a doctor?'

Fleabag yawned and stretched, then turned round twice on the bed and settled down to sleep. 'No,' he said from the depths of his fur. 'Just get on with what you have to do. I'll keep her here.'

Downstairs, Rowanne met the landlord, still peering nervously around the door into the street.

Rowanne held out two silver coins to the man. His eyes lit up. 'These are for you if the girl and the cat are still here when I return.'

The man shot out his hand for the coins.

Rowanne snatched them back into her fist. '*If* they are here when I return.' With that she slipped the money back into her pouch and stepped out into the street.

She was gone less than two hours, but Gemma slept until well into the afternoon. She woke when the chambermaid opened the door and brought in a tray with two bowls of hot stew and a fresh loaf of bread.

'Will you be wanting anything else, Ma'am?'

Rowanne shook her head. 'No. We'll be leaving soon.' The woman curtseyed and shut the door behind her.

Gemma sat up in bed and rubbed her eyes. 'What's happening? What were all the crowds about? I was so frightened.'

'Her Majesty has died,' Rowanne replied simply.

Gemma felt her eyes stinging. 'How can you just say it as if it was the most ordinary thing in the world?' she choked angrily. She wished she could be alone for a while to cry in peace, but the knight was bustling around the room arranging piles of clothes and food into bags. Gemma swallowed hard. She would cry later.

Fleabag saw Gemma was struggling and decided to change the subject. He sprang up onto her bed. 'For once, this . . . cat-hater may have hit upon a good plan.'

'Thank you, mog. I can do my own talking,' Rowanne replied icily. 'Gemma, I have bought a pony for you and some travelling clothes. My horse is already in the stables and I have packed some essentials for us both.

'There is a great deal of unrest in the town: the lack of a named successor seems to have put everyone into a panic. The Prime Minister has declared a curfew at dusk to contain any trouble. I have managed to get permission to leave—but we've got to get on the move as soon as possible in case my captain changes his mind and recalls me to the palace. If that happens it will put paid to all your plans, for you won't get far without me.

'We must go now and ride through the night to be well away from here before dawn.'

'What do you think, Fleabag?' asked Gemma, scratching the cat behind his ears.

'I told you. For once old Miss Full-of-Herself is probably right. Without horses... and an escort, you will travel too slowly and be in too much danger. Whether we like it or not, we need to do exactly as she says... *This* time,' he added quietly, but with emphasis.

Laid out on a chair next to Gemma's bed were riding trousers, a cotton shirt and a squire's leather jerkin. They were rather large and loose and had to be tied with a belt but Gemma could see they would be much more practical for the journey than anything she might have had. Rowanne had put Gemma's own clothes, with the precious green shawl, into a canvas bag.

Once dressed, Gemma began to eat hungrily. Then a thought struck her. 'Fleabag *can* come, can't he?'

The knight stared hard at the cat, who simply smirked back in her direction.

'It seems I can't do much to stop him.'

The cat smirked even more broadly.

Suddenly a thought struck Gemma. 'Why are you doing this? I am an expense to you. Without me, you could have got out of Harflorum hours ago!'

Rowanne felt two pairs of eyes burning into her. She sighed. 'Oh well, you might as well know, I too have a mind to quest for the Queen's Ring. It is very dull at the palace. I was trained for adventure and fighting, not court manners and wearing silk costumes. I have taken leave of absence to find out whether soldiers will be needed to keep the peace in other provinces.'

She did not have the courage to say that the Fire Wielder's words about Gemma having an important message for her, made her think—even hope—that she might be involved in the Ring's finding. Or—perhaps—even find it herself!

She took a deep breath and blurted out very suddenly, so she would not have time to stop herself, 'Let's face it . . . I need you.'

'Ahh!' said Fleabag with immense satisfaction.

'Oh,' said Gemma, with a sinking heart.

'Why does my honesty offend you?' asked Rowanne angrily.

'Because what you are really saying is that I am your prisoner until I can identify the real Ring for you.'

Rowanne was flustered. 'No. No, not at all. You may leave my company any time you choose.'

Fleabag bristled his long, black fur into a huge mane as he sprang onto Rowanne's saddle-bags. 'Swear it!' he demanded.

Rowanne swung a well-aimed kick at Fleabag's head. 'Get off, you louse-infested old hearth-rug!'

But Fleabag ducked and began to dig his claws into the immaculate, richly worked leather of the bags. 'Swear it!' He glowered dangerously through his whiskers. 'Swear it, or I will scratch your posh leather to bootlaces!'

Rowanne narrowed her eyes into piercing blue points. Cat and knight once more began their dangerous game of out-staring each other. But this time, the cat had the added advantage of being able to make tiny little picking sounds on his exalted perch.

After a few seconds, Rowanne risked a glance at Fleabag's claws, poised right over her gold-tooled family crest. She swallowed hard. 'I swear it.' she whispered.

'Louder!' demanded the cat.

'I swear it.'

'Now bind that oath. Swear by your knighthood.'

Rowanne went quite white. 'I can't do that, that's the most sacred oath a knight can make!'

'Exactly!' grinned the cat, flexing his claws a little.

Rowanne looked at Gemma for help, but the girl was clutching her canvas bag and chewing nervously at the corner of it as she edged towards the door. If Gemma reached the door, she would be lost in a warren of backstreet bolt-holes within seconds. There were no crowds outside to delay her now. And if the girl ran, sure as eggs, the cat would follow like greased lightning.

Outside she could hear the town crier calling half an hour to curfew in the streets below. She had to make a decision. She swallowed hard and blurted out, 'I swear by my knighthood that Gemma and

Fleabag are free to leave my company at any time and place of their choosing! But,' she added quickly, 'I also swear by the same oath that I will leave their company whenever I deem it good to do so.'

The room fell silent except for the buzzing of a trapped fly.

'Fine,' said Fleabag cheerfully, jumping down from the saddle-bags. 'That's all I wanted to hear. Come on, Gemma. We must look lively now. Curfew starts soon and we must be well clear of Harflorum by then.'

10

North by North-West!

Horse-riding did not come naturally to Gemma. Fleabag didn't like it much either, but at least he could jump down for a run to stretch his legs occasionally, while Gemma sat like a sack of potatoes on Mistle, the little grey pony.

They had been on the road for only about an hour and a half, but Gemma was already so stiff and tired she kept falling asleep in the saddle. Several times, the knight prodded the girl awake so she would not fall.

Rowanne de Montiland was already deeply regretting having taken Gemma and the cat with her at all. She looked around and sniffed the air. The night would be short and mild. The blossoms on the May trees and wayside daisies glowed almost luminous blue-white in the fast waning light.

What was the best thing to do? She could easily give them the slip in the darkness and leave them. They were still very near home. They could go on or back as they chose. The child could keep the pony and the clothes. What did a few coins matter when so much was at stake? Alternatively, she could force a night ride. The going was good, and they would be well out of her captain's reach by dawn. Or they could just camp for the night and take what came on the morrow.

The girl looked awfully small in her heavy riding clothes, and there was that dreaded cat following close at the pony's heels.

'I was stupid to bring you here,' said Rowanne out loud.

'Perhaps *we* were stupid to bring *you*,' Fleabag retorted.

Rowanne sniffed disparagingly. 'I suppose you two want a rest now?'

'No, my Lady,' Gemma answered timidly. 'I will travel as long as you wish me to.'

Rowanne looked at the thin, tired face. 'We'll see,' she answered curtly. The more distance there was between them and Harflorum, the happier she would be. She would see how long the girl could keep going.

All night they rode steadily, until at the first signs of dawn. Rowanne pulled rein and organized a camp in a clearing not far from the road. Gemma ate some bread and cheese, wrapped herself in a blanket and fell asleep straight away. Fleabag, who had managed to cat-nap on Mistle's back, offered to take the first watch. To his surprise, Rowanne agreed, and she too fell asleep.

He woke them when the sun was quite high. The faint sound of tack jingling had grown steadily closer. Horsemen were approaching. Rowanne buckled on her sword and squatted silently where she could watch the road without being seen herself.

'Why are you acting like this? Anyone would think we were in danger!' whispered Gemma.

'Look first, know later,' said Rowanne curtly. In truth she was still dreading the order to return to Harflorum, but she did not want to admit how much the quest for the Ring had come to mean to her. She merely added: 'There are always thieves about. It pays to be cautious. Hush.'

Gemma felt bemused by Rowanne's behaviour. She shrugged and peered through the undergrowth at the men on the road below. They were only farmers on their way to market. From their talk their only interest was the price of lambs and they soon passed by.

Rowanne suddenly chuckled and slipped her sword back in its scabbard. The captain had more important things to do than to fetch one of the Queen's bodyguards back from what was, after all, a perfectly legitimate mission.

'I think,' she said, 'it will be safe to travel by day. We are quite a way from Harflorum, after all. If we are challenged, however, never say you are on an errand for the late Queen. Simply say I am training you as my new squire. I took you on as a kindness to—your guardian who has recently died. It is all true, and your training would include much riding and learning to survive in the open. Say not a word else . . . especially nothing about the Ring.

'And as for you,' she pointed a threatening finger at Fleabag, 'if you value your fur, say nothing at all. Talking cats are very popular with circuses and I don't think you'd be happy there.'

The party travelled on, keeping the sun at their backs as they rode steadily north by north-west.

Gemma had never left the city before and found the wide open spaces frightening. At first, she kept asking, 'Are we there yet?' It took Rowanne several days to realize that Gemma thought 'north by northwest' was a place, not a direction.

Rowanne tried to explain the rudiments of geography and orienteering, teaching Gemma how to use the sun and a stick as a compass, but quickly realized it was useless. She hoped that they would not meet any of her comrade knights on the road. If they questioned Gemma on her progress, it would quickly become obvious that the child was in no way cut out to be a squire.

Gemma did wonders, however, with camp-fire cooking. And Fleabag was an excellent hunter though he needed to be convinced that rat, vole and fieldmouse were not acceptable on the human menu. Even Rowanne had to give grudging praise to Fleabag's hunting skills.

The first time Gemma was shown how to skin and gut a rabbit, she was sick. After that she pulled herself together. To her surprise she spotted herbs growing wild that she recognized from the palace kitchen. She had never realized before that they came from anywhere other than the market. But Cook had taught her how to stuff thyme and ramsons into the rabbit's carcass, then roast it slowly over a low fire.

Gemma was also amazed to learn that milk came from cows, instead of from churns at the buttery door. Unfortunately, Fleabag could not be dissuaded from helping himself from a milkmaid's pail if he ever found one unattended.

Sleeping arrangements were less successful. Rowanne wanted to avoid the inns. She was worried that anyone talking to the guileless Gemma might guess that the child was somehow important and try to kidnap her. So they slept rough.

Gemma could not get used to always being a little cold, even on mild nights. Neither could she acclimatize herself to finding earwigs and woodlice in her blanket, or even worse, inside her clothes.

Luckily there was not much night rain and they did not get very wet. The local farmers were busy hay-making and were not pleased when lowering skies threatened rain and Rowanne asked if they might sleep in a barn; they were told in no uncertain words that barns were for hay, not for gypsies.

However, Fleabag enjoyed the journey, growing decidedly fat as small rodents fleeing the haymakers ran straight into his paws.

On the eighteenth day, Rowanne seemed particularly jolly and even spared a kind word and a scratch behind the ear for Fleabag. 'My cousin's palace is on the other side of this hill,' she told them at breakfast. 'I think,' she confided, 'there is a very good chance that the Queen's Ring may be there. Then we can all go home and live happily ever after.' She stretched and smiled up at the sun.

Fleabag sniffed the air and twitched his whiskers. 'Trouble ahead,' he said firmly.

'Nonsense!' chided Rowanne. 'It's a lovely day and we'll be sleeping in feather beds by nightfall. I don't know if I'll get you in, you flea-ridden old haybag, but you usually manage to come off best anyway.'

Fleabag twitched his tail contemptuously. 'I still say that all is not well.'

Gemma looked worried and glanced at Rowanne.

'What could go wrong as long as I am with you?' she laughed. 'But if it makes you feel better, I'll keep my sword loose in the scabbard. You're probably just smelling an over-fed rat which has grown to twice your size and is waiting to pounce.'

Fleabag made a face behind Rowanne's back and settled in his usual perch in front of Gemma, with his paws on her saddle pommel. This time, instead of curling up for a snooze, he sat erect, eyes shining and ears pricked.

'It's people!' he whispered at last. 'I smell men, several of them. Their scent has got fear and anger on it,' he added. 'That knight is just too full of herself. Stick close to her, though. I think we're about to see if she's as good as she says she is.'

At that moment, Rowanne caught a tiny glimpse of sun reflecting on metal amongst the trees. It could be a drawn sword . . . or just a woodsman's axe. To be on the safe side, she reached for her little pointed helmet, spread its leather collar around the back of her neck and checked that her dagger was in its sheath at her waist. She decided not to give it to the child. If Rowanne lost her sword, she could still do some damage with the smaller blade, but the girl would just burst into tears and drop it.

The knight sat bolt upright and began to sniff the air like the cat. There was no apparent way around this wood. The road was bordered by a high stone wall on both sides. Either they had to turn back now and expose their backs to danger, or else they must go on.

Rowanne gave her mount a gentle kick in the flanks and began to trot. Gemma did the same to Mistle. The road swung round to skirt the hill in an easterly direction. The morning sun was still low in the sky, catching in their eyes and blinding them for a minute or two as they came to the black shade of the trees.

11

Fleabag the Battle Cat

Rowanne pushed her feet firmly into the stirrups as she braced herself to push her sword deep into the first assailant's throat. He could not scream as he died. He just gurgled as blood and air gushed from the gaping wound.

As she jerked her blade back, she saw another taller, thicker man come rushing at her from behind. She couldn't turn her horse quickly enough to use her sword effectively and she lost a precious second as she reached for her dagger. With a flick of her wrist it came free of its sheath and she caught the man neatly under his ear as he swung his arm back to strike a blow.

The sound of Gemma screaming made her turn her head. One of the men, younger than the others, had Fleabag by the tail and was swinging the howling cat around his head.

Rowanne almost wanted to let him get on with it. He was doing her a favour. But Gemma's sobs made her move. Rowanne lunged under the cat's orbit and caught the man's body with the tip of her sword. As he swung round, heavy with momentum, the blade slashed through his clothes scoring across his chest and back. He hesitated and looked down in horror at the blood began to well and drip in pulsating splashes. As the pain reached his consciousness he lowered his arms and Fleabag bounded free.

In full battle-fury the brave cat then sprang, pouncing upon the last assailant who was trying to pull Gemma from her mount.

The cat clawed his way up the man's back and bit him on the back of the neck. In agony, the robber let go of Gemma and reached for a club which hung from his thick leather belt. Swinging the weapon over his shoulder, thinking that a man stood at his back with several knives, he missed the cat completely.

Instead, the club landed with a sickening thud on the side of Rowanne's head, felling her unconscious on the road.

It was then easy for the man to pull Gemma down and run off into the trees with the horses. It was a good day's haul for him. Two valuable animals, a well-beaten sword and two packs besides. What did it matter that his neck was bleeding and the others had died? All the more for him.

The first thing Rowanne knew was that she felt very sick. She could not think why she felt so ill when she was lying in the woods on such a lovely day. The birds were singing and everything was peaceful. What could possibly be wrong?

She turned her head to the side. It hurt terribly. By her hand, she could see something that looked like a huge cup. Shakily she grasped it. What was it? She knew she ought to recognize it. The object was metal and pointed and had a leather piece riveted to one side. Instinctively she pushed it onto her head. It fitted. A helmet. That was it.

She reached to her hip. Something was missing. Her sword.

Then she remembered everything. She forced herself to sit up and winced. She hurt all over.

Gemma who had been cowering in the shadows came forward gingerly, looking all about her. 'I think they're all gone—or dead.'

She looked at the two men Rowanne had killed and was sick. She had become used to rabbit blood but this was much worse. The younger thief lay quite still. He was bleeding badly and no danger to anyone.

Rowanne shifted her position. She was sitting on something hard. It was her dagger handle. At least she had that.

Fleabag walked unsteadily into Rowanne's painful field of vision. Gritting her teeth she flung the dagger at him.

Somehow he side-stepped it.

'What did you do that for?' he mewed pitifully.

'Wretched beast. If I hadn't tried to save your mangy fur I'd have got them all! Get out of my sight, for by all I hold precious I'll kill you if I ever set eyes on you again!'

Her head hurt too much to try to crawl after the dagger to have another go at killing the cat. She just collapsed backwards and allowed the dizziness to overcome her again.

Gemma took the helmet from the knight's head and loosened her clothing. Then she looked at the wounded robber. He wasn't very old, older than herself, but not yet a full-grown man. He had black down on his face and thick, dark, curly hair. His skin was a rich, clear golden brown. She knew he must be from the southernmost part of the kingdom.

She bent down. Under his skin colour, he was very pale. Without thinking about whether it was right to save the life of someone who had almost killed her best friend, she picked up Rowanne's dagger, ripped his shirt into strips and used it to bind his sword-slash wounds.

When that was done, she felt thirsty. There had been water flasks in their packs, but now they had nothing. They had crossed a stream not far from the entrance to the wood so, picking up Rowanne's helmet, she ran off to fill it with water.

The cool liquid revived Rowanne, and Gemma made a cold compress for the lump on her head with a wetted handkerchief.

The young man groaned when Gemma began to wash his face. At last he regained consciousness and drank, but then both he and Rowanne fell asleep again.

Gemma went back to the stream and washed. To her surprise, Fleabag was there, with all three paws in the water.

'I thought you didn't like swimming,' she said, amazed.

'I don't,' he replied miserably. 'I just can't stand the taste of human blood on my claws.'

Gemma sat on the bank and stroked the cat slowly. 'What are we going to do?' she sighed.

Without answering, Fleabag pounced on an unsuspecting roach and quickly ate it. He shook his fur dry, almost like a dog and stretched out on the grass, washing himself carefully.

'Go on, I suppose.'

'North by north-west?'

'Where else?' replied the cat. 'Are you going to take that ... woman?' he went on. 'She thinks I caused her downfall. I suppose I did, but I couldn't just sit amongst the trees and let her do all the fighting when I have fifteen sharp little daggers and several equally nasty teeth at my disposal. Now she's going to be more insufferable than ever.'

Gemma nodded. 'What's worrying me is that we still need her. One of the thieves is badly wounded, and we ought to try to take him to a doctor. I can't get him to the town on my own. Perhaps we could give her the slip when she goes to see this cousin of hers?'

Fleabag cheered up at this. 'Right, let's get moving, shall we? The day is getting on and I'd like to be away from here as soon as possible.'

When they got back, Rowanne was rousing. Her sickness had passed. She drank more water and noticed with relief that the cat was not around. Then she examined her helmet. It was badly dented where it had taken the brunt of the blow, and without it she would certainly have been dead. She took her dagger and started to clean it on the moss under the trees.

She tried to straighten her clothes, but they were torn and bloodstained. Her only comfort was the thought of dining in Rupertsberg that night with her cousin.

'We'll send Rupert's men back to collect the bodies and see to this one,' she said, pushing her dagger back into its sheath.

'What will happen to him?' asked Gemma shyly.

'Oh, he'll be hanged, I expect,' she said in an off-hand manner, picking bits of wood and moss out of her hair.

'Ladies, I beg a favour,' the young man called weakly.

Rowanne went to him and looked down at him. She did have a sort of grudging respect for anyone who could best Fleabag.

'What is it? I'm not in a very good mood thanks to you and your friends.'

'Lend me your dagger so I can kill myself.'

'You won't have long to live, never fear,' Rowanne laughed.

He coughed, and more blood seeped though the bindings on his body. 'It is fear that I have,' he said. 'I make no secret of the fact that I am frightened of the scaffold. If I crawl into the woods I will die slowly. My fellows will never come looking for me—they daren't risk it: a sick man means slow movement and maybe even a betrayed hide-out. I beg that I may die with dignity of some sort.'

Rowanne crossed her arms and glowered. 'You're a fine one to talk of dignity, with the life you lead—or should I say, led?'

The boy shrugged as best he could. 'What else does an orphan lad do? My parents were unjustly put to death at the orders of that tyrant Prince Rupert. My only friends were the thieves in the shadows. No one else would spare me even a crust.'

Rowanne seethed. 'Prince Rupert is my much-loved cousin, pleb!' she said, kicking him viciously in the ribs. She smiled at the bloodstain on her boot.

Gemma knelt down next to the boy. 'If he is caught, will he stand trial?'

'Of course.'

'Then shouldn't he be well enough to speak in his own defence?' she asked.

'He hasn't *got* any defence,' Rowanne replied curtly.

'What harm did he do you? It was Fleabag he went for!' Gemma ventured.

'Oh yes,' said Rowanne with a delighted grin. 'That's true. But he is still a villain who deserves to die.'

'He is no worse than you. You killed two men today; he killed none. You happen to be the Prince's cousin; he's only an orphan. You're a rich villain who has killed people; he's a poor one who hasn't.' Gemma felt quite exhausted after this speech and sat down hard.

Rowanne looked at her. Her face was hot and flushed with anger. She never much liked being told the truth. 'You sound like that infernal cat!' she said quietly and menacingly. Her dark eyebrows were pulled almost together and her head was thrust forward. She looked as if any second she might go for Gemma's throat.

'Please, I beg you,' whispered the boy on the ground, 'in the mercy of the Fire in Her Majesty's Ring, lend me your dagger and I will be no more bother to either of you.'

At these words, Gemma and Rowanne turned to stare at the boy.

Suddenly Gemma felt again that strange burning in the palms of her hands that the Fire Wielder had

bade her never forget . . . But she *had* forgotten it.
She breathed deeply. She needed all her courage
now Fleabag was not here to speak for her. He would
not be far away, she knew it. But this was *her* battle.

Holding that strange feeling of the burning Ring
Fire clearly in her mind, she curtseyed formally and
bowed her head. 'My Lady Rowanne de Montiland.
I thank you most humbly for your assistance both in
the past and today. If you will grant me one request,
I promise that both I and the cat will be out of your
sight and memory for ever.'

12

At the House of Aelforth

The knight and the child staggered under the weight of the young thief. It did not help that they were so unevenly matched for height. The walk down the hill into the city was not far and it would have taken less than an hour on horseback, but they struggled for the best part of the afternoon.

The lad had told them his name was Phelan, but Gemma was too exhausted to talk to him much, and Rowanne was muttering to herself. She was furious she had been talked into this crazy plan of helping the boy get down to the city, but the thought of being free of all of them for ever was worth the inconvenience—or so she kept telling herself. She carefully avoided thinking of Gemma's role in finding the Queen's Ring.

The city's pale yellow stone walls with open gates gleamed welcomingly in the late sunshine. The guards, wearing Prince Rupert's insignia on their shoulders, did not move from where they lolled as they watched the struggling group approach.

As they crossed the drawbridge, Phelan sank to the ground.

Rowanne stepped up to the sergeant. 'Why did you not run to help us, man? You could see we have a wounded boy here!'

The man laughed in her face. 'What? And get peasants' blood on our uniforms? That's a good one!'

Rowanne propped the boy against the wall and drew herself up to her full height so that she looked down on the soldier. 'I am the Lady Rowanne de Montiland, cousin to your Lord Prince Rupert. We were set upon by thieves, on a road you did not see fit to patrol. Look at this!' She held up her signet ring for the man to inspect, 'My ring bears the de Montiland crest. Now give me your assistance immediately or I assure you my cousin will hear of this!'

The man blanched and called to his fellow. 'Fetch a cart and take these people to the castle. Quick!'

Coldly Rowanne countered, 'Don't worry about them, these peasants are not with me. I met them on the road, they . . . suffered the same fate as I. Out of kindness I helped them reach the town.'

'Forget the cart!' yelled the sergeant over his shoulder. 'Just bring a horse.'

And so Gemma and the young robber watched the Lady Rowanne de Montiland disappear between the houses, mounted and looking very pleased with herself. She did not even turn to wave farewell.

The sergeant scowled at them. 'I suppose you had your money pinched?' Gemma nodded miserably. 'And,' he added wearily, 'I suppose you don't know anyone in the town either?'

Gemma shook her head.

'We don't allow vagrants in this town. You must

go to the hostel for poor travellers. Down there, on the right. House with a green door.' And with that, he turned and started laughing and joking with his companions. Gemma opened her mouth to ask if he could help her get the lad to the hostel, but she could see she had received all the welcome that she was going to get.

A warm push at her legs showed her that Fleabag had slipped in behind them. Remembering that she must not let anyone realize he could talk, she bent down and scratched him behind the ear. 'Hello, Fleabag,' she said. 'Nice to see you, puss.' She would sit and have a heart-to-heart with him later, in private. She still had to apologize to Fleabag for saving the life of his assailant.

The cat sprang onto her shoulder and nuzzled his face into her ear. 'You walk ahead. I'll see where you go and meet you there later,' the cat whispered and with a flick of his tail he had disappeared in the late afternoon shadows.

Gemma watched him go, feeling very lonely. Then she pulled the boy to his feet. 'I know this is going to be hard, but you will have to walk on your own. You can lean on my shoulder, but that is all.'

The two began to struggle down the narrow, smelly backstreet the soldier had shown them. Rubbish and mud clogged the open drain and the air stank.

The boy looked as if nothing mattered to him any more. 'Why didn't you just kill me back there? It would have been better for you and for me. You could have stayed with your mistress and slept in the palace.'

Gemma gave a short, hard laugh. 'I would rather sleep in the gutter than with her in a palace. Anyway, she wasn't my mistress. We were simply going the same way and she looked after me because it suited her.'

The boy nodded. 'I've met people like that.' Laboriously they staggered the length of the lane until they reached the green door. Gemma knocked hard, but there was no reply. She tried the handle, but the door was locked.

She let Phelan sink to the litter-strewn mud and knocked again.

Then suddenly from behind, a rather husky voice asked, 'Can I help you?'

Gemma turned to see a kind-looking man with a spiky, grey beard and wearing a long, homespun robe. In one hand was a large market-bag full of vegetables and in the other a huge iron key.

'It's a good job you came now,' he smiled, opening the door and putting his bag inside. 'Otherwise you would have been locked out until morning. Once I've collected what I can from the market leftovers, I usually bar the door for the night. It looks like this fellow needs a bit of help.' He stooped down, gathered Phelan up in his strong arms and took him indoors.

The hostel was a long, low, stuffy room with straw mattresses pushed closely together all along both walls. Men and women in various states of sickness and poverty sat staring into space or walking in a lost sort of way up and down the room. One or two were doing odd tasks, such as sweeping or peeling potatoes.

The man put Phelan onto a spare mattress. 'Wait here,' he said.

Gemma sat down on a bench and stroked Fleabag who had slipped in as well. The cat gave Gemma a wink and a nod then jumped onto the window-ledge and disappeared into the street.

The man reappeared with a bowl of water and clean rags. He knelt down by Phelan and whistled in amazement as he eased the blood-caked rags from the boy's wounds.

'What happened?'

'We were set upon by robbers on the south road, just where the hill is crowned by woods.'

'I know the place,' said the man. 'It's notorious around here.'

Gemma looked at him. He looked kindly, but she had decided not to trust anyone, especially without Fleabag near. He always seemed to know what people were really like.

'My name is Gemma. I am from the city of Harflorum. My mistress died and I took to the road because I feared ill treatment if I stayed without her protection. I don't know this lad. I think his name's Phelan. He just happened to be ... on the same stretch of road at the same time.'

The man shot her a sharp glance. He must have guessed what she meant. She did not want to lie, but she had no intention of telling the truth either. Anyway, Rowanne was far guiltier than the boy— she was malicious and unfaithful, only concerned with her own comfort and getting the Ring for herself. Gemma hated her at this moment.

'I must tell you I have no money,' she said

quietly. 'But I am a good worker. May I work for our keep until the boy is better?'

The man sat back on his heels and surveyed her. She had clear eyes with a steady look, and her hands were obviously used to work. 'Thank you,' he said. 'That is a good offer. My name is Aelforth, and I am going to need a great deal of help in the next few days to get young Phelan here back on his feet. Now, this water contains salt and will hurt him a great deal, but I must bathe his wounds. You hold his hands so he can't struggle. With any luck, he will remain unconscious while I do it.'

That night, Aelforth would not let Gemma do any work at all. Instead he made her eat and rest to regain her strength.

She lay on a scratchy, thin little mattress and cried. Not because she had been betrayed by Rowanne—she shouldn't have expected much else—but, as much as anything, because she had lost the soft green shawl the Queen had given her.

13

Rowanne Washes Up

Fleabag stretched and rearranged himself under Gemma's chin. She moaned and struggled in her sleep. At last she began to awaken and gave the cat a sharp shove.

'Hey!' came the aggrieved whisper. 'I was comfy there.'

'Well, I wasn't!' Gemma retorted. 'I couldn't breathe with your tail right under my nose!'

'You could at least have asked me to move in a friendly way, instead of shoving me like that!'

'I couldn't talk with all your fur in my face.'

Fleabag stood up and arched his back in a big stretch. Then he sat down, stood up again and turned around twice. At last he settled, face to face with Gemma. She scratched him behind his left ear. 'I owe you an apology,' she said.

'What for?'

'For trying to rescue Phelan, the boy who swung you by the tail. I hope you're still talking to me. I felt I had to do something. No one deserves to be left at the mercy of Prince Rupert... If Her Majesty had known what he was really like...

Oh, but that's all past,' she sighed.

Fleabag licked her nose, then he rolled over on his back, leaving his three legs stuck up in the air at ridiculous angles. Then he began to purr his deep, rolling song. 'I *was* cross at first. But what he did wasn't against me personally, was it? It was the only way he knew how to live. When I heard his life story, I felt he deserved a chance to be different. I might just accidentally use his leg as a scratching post when I see him, but—well, let's see how he turns out before we judge him, shall we? I mean, if he's a decent sort, I might allow him to travel with us, but if he's a baddie then I'll feed him to a particularly unpleasant bulldog I met last night,' and Fleabag turned his head so Gemma could see that yet another chunk was missing from the cat's right ear.

'Wow!' she said. 'Does that hurt?'

'Nah!' sneered the cat. 'Once you've had one chunk taken out of an ear, the rest becomes kitten's play.'

But when Gemma tried to inspect the wound, Fleabag winced and presented his other side to be stroked. 'You're a fraud, cat,' admonished Gemma. 'Tell me if you need something on that.'

'You ought to see the mess I made of the other guy,' grinned Fleabag. 'He'll need quite a lot to soothe *his* aches and pains this morning. By the way, changing the subject to less interesting matters, how is Phelan?'

Gemma sat up, dislodging Fleabag who rolled onto the floor. She peered across the room. 'I can't see from here, but yesterday he wasn't being a very "patient" patient at all. We've been here four days now, and since his fever subsided yesterday morning, he's put all his effort into trying to run away. He doesn't believe that we're not going to turn him over to the authorities. He doesn't trust anyone.'

Fleabag climbed back onto his perch under Gemma's chin. 'Wait until I tell you how Her Ladyship Rowanne Fancypants fared.'

Just then the woman on the next mattress stirred. Gemma pushed Fleabag gently onto the floor. 'Let me get dressed and we'll go outside. I don't want anyone knowing I'm with a talking cat. They'd put you in a cage and that would be the end of your adventures.'

'I'd like to see them try!' said Fleabag as he jumped lightly onto a window-sill. 'See you outside,' he said.

The early morning breeze was very fresh and pleasant. The hot, city smells had not started to clog the air. The garden behind the hostel was used for growing food and hanging washing. Gemma sat in the shade of a dark green plum tree with tiny unripe fruit hanging in swathes above her head. She hugged her knees, her eyes bright with excitement.

The cat was stretched in full sunlight, with his eyes closed, and looking for all the world as if he were asleep. But in reality, he was speaking very, very quietly.

'Well,' he said, 'I have this on excellent authority. There's this very bright little tortoiseshell queen cat in the kitchen. Nice lass. Could get fond of a cat like her . . .'

Gemma twisted his long black fur between her toes and tugged. 'Get on with the story, mog!'

Fleabag took a friendly bite at her foot and settled back to the tale. 'Well, this friend of mine saw the Lady Knight Rowanne de Montiland arrive at the palace gates, looking like something the dog dragged in, but pretending she was the Queen of Sheba... She stuck her pretty little nose in the air and presented her ring to the guards, like she did at the gate...'

Gemma nodded, 'I know! Like this,' and she jumped up and pranced around doing a very neat imitation of the knight.

'But this guard wasn't having any of it. He was a big fat man from the West, with muscles like barrels. He had our friend off her horse and threw her into prison, and I mean threw—down the steps head first, so I hear. This guard reckoned Rowanne was a thief who'd stolen the ring, and had her up on a charge of imitating a member of the de Montiland family, as well as suspected murder of the real Rowanne!'

Gemma leaned back against the tree and laughed. 'Oh, I like it! It serves her right! When's the trial?'

'Yesterday. Some Sheriff who'd never met Rowanne sat in judgment but, because they couldn't get the ring off her finger, he thought there might be a slight possibility she's telling the truth. The mark on her finger shows she's certainly been wearing it for a long time. Still, until her cousin comes back, the Sheriff's condemned her to menial work in the kitchens. It seems they can't keep staff there and so they have all the poor unfortunates doing the greasy jobs about the place!'

Gemma grinned. 'Better and better!'

Fleabag purred contentedly. 'I found the scullery where Rowanne works. She was washing up all day. I sat on a window-ledge where I could see it all. I could have watched her for hours. I smiled and waved a paw of course, and she saw me, but she didn't seem to appreciate it. She threw a dishmop at me. That's the last time I'll try and be friendly to her!'

Gemma rolled over so she lay next to Fleabag on the warm grass. 'Meanwhile,' she said. 'I need you to do some thinking. People are only allowed to stay here for a week. They say it prevents anyone becoming dependent on the place or something. Anyway, Aelforth who's in charge says that's stupid. He gets people well and clean and almost ready to be able to go out and look for work, then the rules say he has to turf them out and they can't come back for a month. By the time people are allowed to come back, after sleeping rough all that time, they're ill and dirty again.'

'Who makes the rules?'

'Prince Rupert, of course. Anyway, a sergeant comes round every day and checks the entries, and makes sure the rules are followed. We're only going to be allowed to stay three more days—that's two more nights. What are we going to do? Are we going to try and take Phelan with us? His gang won't take him back. And what do we do about Rowanne? Should we try and rescue her?'

'Why should we?' snapped Fleabag. 'We promised her she'd never hear from us again.'

'I suppose, like Phelan, she's a human being who needs help.'

'Call that a "human being"?' sneered Fleabag.

Gemma looked serious. 'Well, it's more that she was sort of given to us to look after, by the Fire Wielder, if you remember. I get the feeling we are meant to stick together.'

Fleabag stopped purring and took a lazy swipe at a butterfly that came too close. 'Ummm,' he said doubtfully.

'I think she ought at least to have the choice—she ought to know we're here if she needs us. And that we're leaving on . . . let's see . . .' she counted on her fingers, 'Thursday.'

Fleabag said, 'Ummm,' again, even more thoughtfully. He twisted his head round so he could see her properly and said, 'You look sort of Ring Fire-ish at times—and this is one of them.'

Gemma rubbed at the palms of her hands. They *did* tingle rather. She just said, 'This window you saw her near, is it one I could talk to her through? You'd better not get near her in case she cuts one, if not all three, of your other legs off.'

The window where Rowanne worked was barred and bolted, but a small pane was propped open for the scullerymaid to throw vegetable peelings and bones out into the streets below. The heap of rotting rubbish under the window was slippery and evil-smelling. Fleabag climbed it lightly. He paused halfway up to whisper encouragement to his friend. Then, at the sight of a slim tortoiseshell cat rounding the corner, he was away.

Nervous and sickened by the smell, Gemma climbed to the top and peered over the sill. A woman was working at the sink, scrubbing pans. She was dressed in a none-too-clean peasant's dirndl. Her black hair was plaited in two braids and tied back in a greasy grey kerchief. Gemma knocked at the window, and a cross face looked up. It was Rowanne.

Gemma smiled. 'Are you OK?'

Rowanne scowled. 'No, I am *not*. No one could be all right in this hell hole. Anyway, how did you know I was here?'

'Fleabag knows one of the kitchen cats.'

Rowanne made a face. 'Don't mention that animal's name to me... ever!' and she waved a bread knife wildly. Then she leaned over close to the window. 'Anyway, Rupert comes home tonight, and I'm to be brought before him.'

Suddenly there was a bellowing like a cow in pain, and a clatter of dishes being thrown or dropped.

'Quick, duck! Here comes the chief kitchenmaid. She's a fat pig and I hate her!'

For a few moments Gemma squatted on the heap of rotting vegetables and listened. She only heard a rough angry voice, and the clatter of more iron pots being put ready to wash.

'All clear!' whispered Rowanne.

Gemma leaned close to the window. 'Listen, I can only stay here two more nights, then I get chucked out of the hostel. I don't know what I'm going to do, so I'll be on my way, I suppose. Will you come too?'

Rowanne looked worried. She remembered she needed Gemma to identify the Ring. She made a conciliatory face. 'I'm sure I could get you a job and somewhere to sleep in the palace...?'

'No, thank you!' said Gemma with an inward shudder.

Suddenly a passing soldier yelled, 'Oi you, no begging at palace windows. Move along before I arrest you for vagrancy!' He picked up a rotten potato and lobbed it in her direction.

'If all goes well, I will send for you tomorrow!' called Rowanne, as Gemma slithered down the pile and ran for her life.

14

Fleabag Plays Marbles

Dinner with Prince Rupert was a grand affair at the simplest of times. Bathed and dressed for the occasion, Rowanne looked quite the part. She preferred the court dress of a lady knight to the flowing frills of a lady-in-waiting: rose silk pantaloons with white silk stockings, white satin shoes, a vermilion shirt and a white tabard with Prince Rupert's crest. Her long dark hair was loose over her shoulders and smelled of lavender.

She smiled as the guard who had arrested her was sentenced to ten years' hard labour. She dabbed at her pink lips with a damask serviette and nibbled at a little of the fruit set before her.

The man was led away, howling protests that he was only doing his duty and that he had a wife and children to support.

'Oh, very well,' yawned the Prince. The man turned with a look of relief on his face. 'Let them do ten years hard labour as well, then they can stay together.'

Rowanne closed her eyes for a second and imagined a picture of a lonely, frightened family. She winced involuntarily.

Rupert turned and bowed slightly to his beautiful cousin Rowanne de Montiland. He mistook her pale look of horror for anger.

'My dear cousin, does that not please you? How else can I beg your forgiveness for the terrible treatment at the hands of these ill-bred, misbegotten thugs I am forced to employ!'

Rowanne laughed lightly, but a tiny scratch caught at her silken stocking. She brushed it away. 'Consider it never happened. *Dear* Rupert, it is so good to see you. I can forgive any misunderstanding.'

'Should I have had him hanged?' the Prince mused, leaning on a thin hand and tossing a sweet white grape into his mouth.

Rowanne remembered the terrified thief boy looking up at her, begging not to be sent to the scaffold.

Just at that moment, two claws caught at her stocking and scratched her leg. It was that infernal cat!

She dropped her napkin on purpose and stared into Fleabag's accusing golden eyes.

'If you don't go away, I'll scream, and I'll have you flayed alive for clawing me!'

'No, you won't,' smirked the cat. 'You know perfectly well that a cat saved the Prince's life when he was little, and the attention of a cat is considered the highest honour in this palace.

'I'll think of something,' she assured him, and he smirked back at her.

'No, don't hang the man,' she said to Rupert. She hesitated. 'It was just a mistake, after all.'

The Prince lifted a thin, dark eyebrow and plucked at the bunch of grapes. 'Very well,' he lifted a hand to dismiss the soldiers.

A full set of claws now tore at Rowanne's stocking. She jumped. 'Er, he *was* only trying to do his job. It was not his fault—he had never seen me before and I was dirty and ragged after the fight . . . could he not just be . . .' the first set of claws on her leg was joined by more on her other leg . . . 'Could he not just lose rank and be sent back to work?' she ventured. She was not even sure it was her own voice speaking, but as the words were out, one set of claws lessened their torture.

Prince Rupert looked amazed. 'Oh, very well,' he yawned, 'I'm tired of all this.'

Rowanne smiled warmly. 'I do think your judgments are so *wise*, dear cousin.' At that moment, the second set of claws disentangled themselves from her leg, and a soft, warm feeling engulfed her feet in a comforting wrap as Fleabag began to purr loudly. The man was marched out of the room and the Prince smiled back at Rowanne. He loved flattery. 'I was wanting to talk to you anyway, dear cousin. I have much to discuss.'

'So have I.' She put her head on one side. She could feel the cat bracing himself for an attack if she spoke one word out of place. Why had she let herself be bullied by him? She wouldn't let it happen again.

The purr grew louder.

'What is that noise?' asked the prince.

'Oh,' Rowanne hesitated. 'There's a . . . cat under the table. I was just stroking him!' At the lie a sharp claw picked at her already sore leg.

'How nice,' the prince replied. 'I know how you used to dislike cats. It has been that which has prevented me from speaking out what burns within my heart... dear cousin, will you marry me? Now you have been honoured by a palace cat, I feel sure it is a sign that you will say yes...'

Rowanne blushed and went white in turns. This was the last thing she had expected. Before the Queen's death, she might have said yes, but now, things were different.

'My Prince, what can I say? It is such an honour! Before I can answer you, I must tell you something very important... something that may have a bearing on your request.'

'Speak on, my dear. We must have no secrets if we are to be wed.'

Rowanne swallowed hard and began to tell a very edited version of what had brought her to the city. In her story, she told how the Queen herself had sent her on this mission to find the Ring... and that should she, or even he find it, then they would be King and Queen of the entire land, not just Prince and Princess of the province.

The Prince's eyes opened wider and wider with delight, for he was every bit as ambitious as his cousin. He had heard of the quest, of course—every street corner was buzzing with gossip about it. As a relative of the late Queen, he had been officially invited to take part. But although he was greedy, he was also lazy. Consequently he was, as he told Rowanne, 'still thinking about it'.

Suddenly he sat up straight and clapped his hands to summon his valet. 'Call the palace jeweller,' he demanded. 'And make sure he brings me every box of trinkets I possess. I wish my intended bride to choose an engagement ring for herself,' he said with a broad wink. 'It must be very special. I think she should have . . . an opal.'

The poor jeweller spent long hours, deep into the night, bringing box after box of rings to his royal master. But there were very few with opals. With downcast eyes (for he feared for his neck) he informed the Prince and the Lady, 'There's been a bit on a run on opals since the Queen's death. It's funny,' he mused, 'no one seemed to like them much before.'

Time and time again he was sent back to the treasury to open more safes and rummage through ancient chests and boxes. At last, with relief and delight, the grey little jeweller presented a ring with three magnificent opals held in eagles' claws. But Rowanne still shook her head. 'I fancy,' she said with a look at the Prince, 'one with a simple band, and perhaps just one, large opal . . . with a fire in it.'

The jeweller looked frightened, for he understood the significance of what she had said. 'I am very tired now,' yawned Rowanne. 'But in the morning, I will draw what I have in mind for you.'

The jeweller bowed, 'Very good, Ma'am. A drawing will help a great deal. If you will forgive me, I will go and look through my stock of raw stones immediately to see what can be polished and mounted for your pleasure.'

The prince waved his dismissal and the terrified little man scurried out of the room.

Rowanne yawned again and smiled knowingly at the prince. He nodded. She was clever. Very clever. He admired that. She would be a very useful consort.

Then she said, 'If I am to stay here, dearest, I would very much like my personal maid sent for. We were—separated at the gates when the misunderstanding took place. I heard tell she is at the poor traveller's hostel. Her name is Gemma Streetchild. I do not want the girl frightened, for she is new to my service and timid, so do not send for her until the morning. Would you mind if I retired now?—dearest . . .'

The Prince rose and bowed as she left the room. He blinked and wondered at the huge tears in her new silk stockings and the blood which trickled down to her shoes from raw claw marks . . .

Gemma Streetchild was not to be found when a servant from the Palace came to the hostel in the morning. For once, even Fleabag did not know where she was.

Aelforth just shook his head when the servant questioned him. 'The people come and the people go. They have no homes or addresses. If I asked them questions they would have no answers.'

He shrugged, and watched the servant step gingerly past the rows of elderly and frail guests. Aelforth stroked his greying beard and wondered how he could warn the girl. The place would be watched now, and he did not trust whatever was afoot.

He turned to start his morning rounds of the sick. It was then he realized that the boy, Phelan, was gone also. That troubled him, for there was something about the lad which was familiar . . .

Gemma had got up early to sit in the garden while the air was still cool and the streets were quiet. As she had passed by the beds where the sick lay, she too had discovered that Phelan was missing.

She slipped out of the back door and climbed the garden wall. Sitting on top, she could see along the street in both directions. Cat-like she jumped down on the other side and made for the town gate. It was still bolted. All the gates would be locked at this hour; it was scarcely dawn. He must still be in the city, but he had no friends or family—unless he knew some thieves, he must be hiding. Why had he run away when there was nothing to run away *from* and nowhere to go *to*?

She felt sad, hurt and a little lonely. She had not got to know Phelan well—he hardly said anything— but she wished him no harm. He had found life tough and he had grown up having to fight all the way, but he was nice enough for all that. Apart from Fleabag, he was her only friend.

Tomorrow she and the cat must leave the city and go north by north-west, on their own. She would have been glad of someone else to talk to—someone who wouldn't sneer at her all the time—someone who would not bring in dead rats before breakfast . . .

Slowly she wandered back to the hostel and walked straight into the arms of Rowanne's messenger. There was no use denying who she was. Aelforth looked like a man who could never lie and the shock on her own face was enough to betray herself.

She changed out of the hostel smock she had been loaned and put on her own clothes which had been washed and mended. Gemma asked leave to thank Aelforth, and took the chance to whisper: 'He left very early. I don't know where he is.' She glanced at Phelan's empty bed and Aelforth nodded. The servant had asked nothing about the boy, and it was probably best he had gone before any connections between the two were made.

Gemma was given a small neat attic room. As the personal maid to the Prince's supposed fiancée she was given a pretty blue dress and treated almost civilly.

As soon she had bathed and made herself presentable, Gemma was sent for. She was shown into Prince Rupert's library, where Rowanne sat at one side of a huge desk and the tall, thin, hook-nosed prince at the other. Gemma did not like the look of him. He appeared hard and cynical.

Spread on the table were hundreds and hundreds of rings. Some had opals, others had large round stones of other hues. In the corner cowered a small, grey little man with a huge watch-glass in his right eye. He looked for all the world like a rather moth-eaten old owl.

'My maid may not look like much'—she hesitated, the girl did look better nicely dressed—'but she has a very good idea of the engagement ring I fancy. Come here, child . . . Gemma approached her, but stood carefully at a respectful distance. Rowanne shot out an arm and pulled her closer. She thrust a pencil and paper into her hand, and said, 'Draw! Draw me the ring I have always hankered for, *dear* girl!' She reinforced her demand with a sharp kick from under the table with a new, long, leather, cat-proof boot.

Gemma felt her eyes stinging with tears. What could she do? She picked up the pencil and began to draw. How could she make it look enough like the royal Ring to fool Rowanne, but not enough to betray the Queen?

Just then with a magnificent rumbling purr, Fleabag appeared and jumped onto the table. With kittenish glee he began to roll the rings around and pat them with his paws, sending them skimming across the room in cascades of glittering delight.

'Oh my rings! My gems!' squealed the jeweller as he bent his rheumaticky little knees and began to gather the stones into numerous leather bags which he pulled from every pocket.

At first, Prince Rupert began by being playful with Fleabag, but soon realized that the stones were rolling away and being lost between the floorboards.

Rowanne went quite white. That cat must be got rid of! But easier said than done. Her fingers itched to do the animal real damage.

Having pounced and danced across the table, sending papers and gems everywhere in a lively scramble, Fleabag then leapt onto the floor and skittishly skidded here and there across the polished boards, playing croquet with the crystals and marbles with the margarics. The moonstones he potted into mouseholes under the skirting boards.

Gemma crawled under the table in a pretence of helping to pick everything up. But instead she gently flicked the stones past the cat for him to pounce on.

After several minutes of this, even Prince Rupert no longer found the cat's antics amusing and Rowanne had found a sword. The knight lowered her dark eyebrows and cornered the cat, head down, every muscle in her tense body ready to pounce and slice Fleabag in two.

But Prince Rupert intervened. 'Don't kill the cat, my dear, he's only a poor dumb animal after all . . .'

Rowanne turned on the Prince and glowered. She opened her mouth, thought better of it and shut it again. After all, she had need of the Prince's good-will.

'Take the cat away, Gemma, and put him in the kitchen. Then come back here and clear up this mess.' Fleabag nestled contentedly in his friend's arms and stuck out his tongue at Rowanne as he was carried past.

Rowanne bristled but could do nothing except put up her sword. She had to keep Rupert's trust.

Gemma spent the whole day on her knees gathering up loose gems and rings of every imaginable shape and size. The next day, carpenters came to take up the floorboards and remove the skirting boards, until every last stone was found. Gemma drew a likeness of the Queen's ring, but she comforted herself with the thought that the quality of stone could never be matched—and the fire was unlike anything else that had ever burned in all the world. No jeweller on earth could even begin to imitate it.

It was thus that Gemma found herself employed at the palace, with no prospect of resuming her travels for the time being at least. For a while it did not seem to matter very much. The summer was still young, and a royal palace seemed as good a place as any to begin looking for the Queen's Ring.

Her duties were to supervise the care of Rowanne's extensive new wardrobe of clothes and to clean her suite of rooms. But in her spare time, Gemma was sent out with a team of girls to 'spring-clean' the palace. Her task was to check in every nook and cranny in case, by any chance, the Queen's Ring had been hidden there.

This she did not mind. After all, she too wanted to find the Ring, if only to make sure that Rowanne did not.

Fleabag wandered around at will and kept Gemma informed of all the gossip. One day, he had rather exciting news.

15

Gemma Speaks Out

'You remember I told you about Tabitha, the nice little tortoiseshell queen in the kitchen?' Fleabag rolled over on his back and smirked. Gemma scratched his tummy.

'Well, she's a good sort, is Tabitha. She told me something very interesting indeed. She says that about the time the Queen died, three black ravens landed on the palace roof. Now she likes the tiles, does Tabitha, we've often spent an evening up there... Anyway, she was about to try and catch a raven for supper, when she heard them talking.

'The first one said, "Here! Let's put it here. A king or queen is bound to find a royal Ring in a royal palace—where better to find the new sovereign of our land?"

'But the second raven shook his head and said, "No, no. True royalty lies in wisdom, not in palaces and soldiers. A king may live in a palace, but without wisdom, he is no king at all."

'It was then Tabitha saw that one raven carried a large opal ring in its mouth.

'She was so amazed that she did not pounce

quickly enough. The ravens smelled her near and flew off!'

Gemma picked Fleabag up and nuzzled his warm fur. His whole body shook gently with his deep purr.

'What are we going to do, cat?' she asked quietly. 'We have been here many weeks now. The summer is almost gone and in the market-place people are beginning to lose hope that the Ring will be ever be found. I should have guessed that the Ring would not be hidden anywhere belonging to such an unwholesome creature as Prince Rupert.' She shivered in disgust. 'Rowanne is unofficially betrothed to the man and it looks as if I am going to be kept here for ever.'

The cat dropped to his feet and started to examine a few itchy places under his fur. 'At least the fleas die off in winter and I'll be a bit more comfortable for a while,' he mused.

Gemma took no notice. 'The Prince said something the other day about what would happen if the Ring were never found. I didn't understand it, but I didn't like it either. Something about seeing who was and wasn't fit to rule and getting his soldiers ready for a fight . . . Is this what will happen if the Ring Fire goes away?'

'I guess so,' replied the cat. Then he rolled over on his back. 'Scratch my tummy again!' he demanded.

Absent-mindedly Gemma did as she was told. 'Rowanne will never leave here. She has it made whatever happens next. Prince Rupert was the old Queen's nephew and Rowanne is his cousin. If the Ring isn't found, they will be the obvious choices for the throne. Especially if they are married.'

'What does the Ring Fire tell you?' purred Fleabag unexpectedly.

'The Ring Fire? I get a burning pain in my hands, if that's what you mean. I know I've got to do something fairly soon. But I'm scared . . . even with a mighty cat like you by my side. Humans . . . well . . . need humans. But I know it is time we went on again—north by north-west—with her or without her.'

The cat rolled over and sat bolt upright. He looked at Gemma. 'You must tell Rowanne your thoughts. You are right, she was sent to be with us. We need her—if she will come. If she has the choice, and refuses, then you and I will set off together. When will you have the chance to speak with her alone?'

Gemma put the cat down and leaned out of the window. The tower clock showed five o'clock. 'In about an hour, when I dress her for dinner.'

'Good!' Fleabag announced. While you wait, get yourself packed and organize yourself some food for the journey. I've got a few goodbyes to say myself.' And with that, the grinning cat slipped out of the room.

Gemma looked around. She had packed like this once before. She pulled out the squire's clothes she had arrived in: trousers, shirt and leather jerkin. She held them up. They did not seem as big as when she first wore them. She had grown and filled out while she had been at the palace. She looked at herself in the mirror. Her cheeks were pinker and rounder and her freckles had become alarmingly brown and multitudinous in the summer sun.

Her mousy hair was well brushed and tied back in a long plait that came halfway down her back. She straightened her blue dress. It was prettily made, with a white lace collar. It was the sort of thing she would have treasured before, but it would not fit her soon. Anyway, with winter approaching a cotton dress would be of no use whatsoever.

Instead she took out more trousers and a woollen jacket. The leather shoes the Queen had given her still fitted well. She had no winter coat, so she pulled a thick blanket from her bed and rolled it up tightly. She would need it at night and it could be a cloak by day.

Gemma glanced at the clock. Just time to grab something from the kitchen. If she told them she had to go on an errand for her mistress (which was true, she was still on the Queen's quest) they would allow her to take what she pleased.

At six o'clock she knocked on Rowanne's door. Of late the knight had taken to wearing the flowing robes of a courtly lady. They were fiddly and difficult to fit. Dressing Rowanne often took at least an hour and then her hair and make-up had to be ready in time for dinner at eight. Gemma thought all of this an extraordinary waste of time, but it meant she would have about half an hour alone with Rowanne before the hairdresser came.

When she went into the room, Rowanne was sitting at her dressing table in a cream satin under-slip. Gemma curtsied and went to the wardrobe. 'What would you like to wear this evening, Ma'am?'

Rowanne did not look up. 'The turquoise blue. The jeweller has at last made a ring that looks . . .

109

right!' Rowanne smiled at herself in the mirror. The look was unpleasant and triumphant.

'Tonight, the Prince and I will announce our engagement and I will wear the Ring of the Land.'

She held out her strong fingers and imagined the pale, fiery-hearted opal already there.

Gemma stumbled on the hem of the turquoise silk dress. She did not know what to do with the feelings that rushed through her or the terrible burning pain in her hands. She covered up her clumsiness with a curtsey. 'Congratulations, Ma'am!' she mumbled.

Rowanne swung round and glared at Gemma. 'You're not really pleased, are you?' she snapped.

Gemma closed her fists to hide the Ring Fire. It burned so fiercely that she almost expected to see the flame.

Since Rowanne had been living at the palace, she had become alarmingly selfish, like her cousin. Now her dark-browed eyes narrowed as fury built up. Gemma found she was frightened. But something had to be said. Now. The Fire Wielder was depending on her.

Suddenly she made herself open her hands so the fire could burn if it wished.

'No, Ma'am, I'm not happy. Just look at yourself—all dressed in frills and laces like a courtier. You're not being true to yourself. You'll never be happy here!'

Rowanne shrugged. 'It's all a means to a very useful end.'

Gemma felt the Ring Fire burning even more strongly. 'And *what* end is that? It's not the real Ring—neither will it be the real Fire. I think you'll have precious little joy from either of them and you'll never forgive yourself if you go through with this nonsense. If you'll take my advice, you'll throw away those silly clothes you're wearing and come north by north-west with me. Tonight!'

Rowanne had her head down. Her nostrils were flared and she was flushed. The fury in her face was plain to see. With her right hand she toyed with the handle of her dagger. 'Get out of my room. Immediately!' she said very quietly and dangerously.

Gemma turned and fled. As the door slammed behind her, there was a heavy thud as a dagger hit the wood.

'Well,' said Fleabag consolingly, 'she can't have wanted to kill you very much . . .'

'Why's that? asked Gemma as she ran up the servants' stairs two at a time.

'Because,' puffed Fleabag as he flung himself into her room and landed on her bed, 'the Lady Knight Rowanne de Montiland does not have a reputation for missing her mark.'

Gemma flung her blue dress onto the bed, changed into her travelling clothes and grabbed her bundle. Within seconds, she was shutting the bedroom door behind her. But for one moment she hesitated.

'What's the matter?' asked Fleabag.

'It's just—well, I always wanted a room of my own. It's what I longed for more than anything else in all the world. And now it's gone.'

But then she heard steps approaching. In case it was a guard coming to arrest her, Fleabag led her to the stepladder which went up to the top attic. Then they ventured out onto the climbing boards that the roof repairers used to check the slates. 'Don't look down,' he warned. 'It's quite safe for humans. I've often seen men with hammers spend all day up here.'

'I'm not a man with a hammer,' whispered Gemma, trying to keep her eyes on Fleabag's bottle-brush tail ahead.

At last the boards sloped down to a window above another part of the palace that Gemma had never seen before. The wall was thickly covered with ivy. Fleabag sprang lightly between the leaves, but Gemma found it more difficult. Not least because the ivy branches were brittle, shaking and snapping under her weight.

'Throw your bundle down,' the cat whispered. 'Then you'll have two hands.'

Gemma did as she was told and quickly joined Fleabag on the ground.

Swiftly they ran through the kitchen garden and out of the wicket gate at the back. Fleabag went ahead to see if he could find any soldiers. Then with a flick of his whiskers, he called her on. Trying to look as normal as possible they wandered through the backstreets of Rupert's city.

Gemma was worried. It would be dark soon and the gates would close. She would have been glad of a night's sleep before travelling. Facing a night alone—or almost alone outside the city walls was frightening enough . . . But which way was north by north-west?

It was then a firm hand gripped her shoulder.

16

Autumn and Porridge

They entered a tiny, hot room, with a very old lady seated by an open fire, stirring a pot. She looked just like a witch.

Gemma was pushed forward, nearer to a candle that burned on the table. She turned to glare at her captor. He was a tall, dark-skinned young man from the South. His beard was thin and his eyes were smiling.

Gemma gasped with delight and gave him a hug. 'Phelan! I'm so glad you're all right!' she said.

'Who've you brought in this time, youngster? Another waif and stray, or is it a spy?' the old woman croaked though empty gums.

'Auntie, this is the girl who saved my life—I told you about her,' explained Phelan.

'What's she doing here?' snapped the old lady.

'I brought her here. She looked frightened.'

The old woman snorted contemptuously.

'I *was* frightened,' Gemma admitted. 'But worst of all, I've lost my cat, he was in the street with me. I'd be a lot happier if he was here too.'

'If you mean this one,' said Auntie, kicking a black

lump of fur with her toe, 'he seems to have found his own way in.' Sure enough, there was Fleabag, stretched out in front of the fire, toasting his paws.

'Yes, that's him. Everything's all right now.'

'Is it really?' asked Phelan. 'You looked worried sick when I saw you in the street.'

'I was,' she said. Then pushing her fears aside, she told them the whole story.

Auntie scratched her hairy chin as she listened. 'There is good in the tale which I will not gainsay. She can sleep the night in front of the fire. But I have some advice.'

Gemma looked up expectantly. The old lady passed over a rusted pair of scissors. 'Cut your hair. The prince's soldiers are looking for a girl. You've got a lad's clothes already, but your hair betrays you. Close to, you'd never pass as a boy and your voice is all wrong, but if you shut your mouth and keep out of the way, there's a chance you might win through. In the morning the lad will help you slip out of the city unseen and set you on the road.'

With that the old crone slopped greasy stew into bowls. When they had all eaten, she climbed stiffly up the stairs to her bed.

When they were alone, Gemma whispered, 'I'm glad you found your Auntie. I thought you had no relatives.'

Phelan laughed out loud. 'This is a thieves' hide-out. She's sister, mother and aunt to us all! Now, you will need a proper night's sleep if you're going on the road. Good night.' Then Phelan slipped out of the room too, leaving Gemma and Fleabag alone.

Before dawn the boy reappeared and led Gemma silently through the dim streets to an easily climbed part of the wall where no guard stood.

Phelan pointed out the road and turned to go.

'Won't you come with me?' she begged. 'Even with Fleabag, I can't pretend I'm not frightened.'

Phelan shook his head and laughed. 'What have rogues and criminals to do with the Fire in the Ring? I would put it out as soon as look at it!'

Gemma felt the slight burning in the palms of her hands. 'No, you wouldn't. Not you!' she added with conviction. But he had already gone, so sadly she picked up her bundle and followed Fleabag down the fallen stones and onto the road.

The first few days passed comfortably enough, until the food ran out. Fleabag caught a rabbit, but Gemma could not cook it as she had neither knife to clean it nor tinder box to make a fire. She quickly found that too many nuts and berries made her stomach ache, so she survived by offering to scrub floors and do washing for farmer's wives, in exchange for a night's shelter and a square meal. The farmers were happier to give barn room now the hay and the harvest were safe. Perhaps too, they felt less threatened by a child and a cat than by a formidable knight.

Gemma soon learned to cope with this strange way of life, although she often had the feeling she was being watched or followed. But the leaves had turned rich gold and were falling fast. Autumn was coming to an end. The winds were beginning to blow cold. She was halfway though the year and a day allowed to find the Ring. She was quite alone in a strange part of the land, and she did not even really know whether she was doing the right thing or not.

Slowly but surely the days grew colder and Gemma's progress slowed. One night she had no work and no sheltering barn. Her blanket was damp and smelly from heavy rain and she felt ill. A shepherd's storm shelter kept the wind off her back, and Fleabag did his best to keep her warm. But it was a long, miserable night.

At first light, Fleabag brought Gemma two harvest-fed rats, but his efforts were not appreciated.

Gemma peered over the blanket with feverish eyes. 'I need water, but you can't carry it. Oh, I feel so sick.' Then she pulled the blanket up over her head and fell asleep.

Fleabag climbed up a dry-stone wall to watch the road for passers-by. He would just have to risk being identified as a talking cat. If Gemma did not get help soon, she would become very ill. She needed humans and cups of water and warm blankets. This was no time to think about what life might be like in a circus. He would just have to talk his way out of that one if it came to it.

He sat on the wall all morning. One farmer's lad gave Gemma a drink, but no one seemed to want to take her home. As night began to fall and the cold wind began to whip up the remaining autumn leaves into a dancing frenzy, a dark shape appeared on the road.

As Fleabag watched, the one shape split into two and then three. It was a man on horseback leading two ponies. Fleabag balanced indecisively on the wall. Something about the figure made him nervous. Should he run and hide, or stay and beg help?

He glanced inside the shelter. Gemma was shivering violently.

Plucking up all his courage, as the horses drew level Fleabag balanced himself and took a flying leap, right onto the pommel of the rider's saddle.

The rider jumped. He had obviously dozed off in the saddle. The horse snorted and swung round.

A deep woman's voice swore roundly. 'Fleabag, you wretched animal, you'll be the death of me if I'm not the death of you first!'

'Trust me to pick on *your* horse when I need real help. I'll go away and find someone I can trust,' and he tried to leap down.

Rowanne de Montiland's firm hand grasped Fleabag by the scruff of his neck. She reined in the horse and looked the cat in the eye. 'Listen, don't judge me by what you think you know. Where is Gemma? What's the matter?'

Fleabag knew that even Rowanne's help was better than none. 'Let me breathe and I'll show you,' he said, making it sound as if she were about to strangle him.

She let him go and sprang out of the saddle after him.

Within minutes, she had Gemma wrapped in dry blankets and astride the horse in front of her. Fleabag chose a gap between two bundles on the back of one of the ponies and they headed off up the road.

At the next farm, the farmer's wife regarded Gemma's fever suspiciously. Autumn fever was a dreaded illness. But she changed her mind at the sight of gold.

For three days, Rowanne sat by Gemma's bed, feeding her sips of water and gruel. For four nights, Fleabag watched, curled up at the end of his friend's bed, dozing lightly and opening an eye at Gemma's slightest sound.

On the fourth day she got up and ate well. She was still weak, but as she sat wrapped in rugs next to the farm fire, Rowanne told her what had happened since they had left Rupertsberg.

The night Gemma ran away, Rowanne had pleaded illness and sat alone in her room for a whole night and a whole day.

While she was alone, she began to see that Gemma and Fleabag had been right. Rupert was unjust and greedy, oppressing his people and helping no one except himself.

The next day, she made up a story that she had dreamed that the Ring Fire spoke to her, telling her she was not to marry until she had completed her quest—one way or the other—and that she must set off straight away. After many angry scenes and much persuasion, she convinced Rupert that the real Ring must be hidden in a place shown to her in her dream.

Better, she argued, to have one more go at finding the real thing, than to look foolish with the imitation. If the real Ring was not to be found, then they stood a good chance with the new one.

Rupert, who was cunning but not very clever, finally agreed and equipped Rowanne with an entourage of mounted soldiers, travelling clothes and money for the journey. But he refused to act quickly, taking as long as possible over everything. At last all was ready, but Rupert still would not let

Rowanne leave until he had celebrated his birthday feast. She stayed, but only because she needed the supplies and the gold he had given her.

At last, with smiles and kisses she pushed the imitation ring onto Rupert's little finger so hard it would never come off again, and waved goodbye to Rupertsberg.

At first she had led her escort onto the southern road, then after two days, she got them drunk and slipped away unnoticed. Walking a horse and two ponies along the bed of a stream so they could not follow her tracks, she came north, travelling only by night and leaving false trails here and there.

For once, she seemed to be genuinely glad to see Fleabag, although her legs still bore the scars of long scratchmarks under her knee-high boots.

Fleabag treated her with caution. The sixth sense in his whiskers told him that she had betrayed them before, and although she seemed to have changed, she could betray them again.

The next day Gemma was well enough to travel and they set off. Rowanne gave her the plump little grey pony called Porridge and Fleabag rode perched on a pannier. The land was a wide, open plain, and the wind whistled mercilessly across the emptiness. The trees were now stripped quite bare and the days were very short. Ice formed on the horses' water pails in the morning and more and more often at night they tried to find a farm or inn where they could sleep.

'I've been thinking,' said Rowanne one morning. 'It's only a short detour from the road to the university town of Porthwain. It is still very much north by north-west of Harflorum, so we aren't really going out of our way... What better place to hide the symbol of kingship than in the seat of wisdom? It must be there. We will ask at the university!'

Fleabag and Gemma looked at each other. They had not reported what Tabitha had heard the ravens saying.

'Oh, great!' yawned Fleabag. 'You'll just go up to one of the professors and say, "Anyone here got the Queen's Ring? Can we have it? Thanks!"'

Gemma gave his ear a quick tweak. 'Don't be rude!' she whispered. 'I don't want to get Rowanne's back up. I'm afraid we need her.'

Taking an easterly turning at the next crossroads, another day's ride brought them within sight of the walls of Porthwain. As it was no military base, the 'walls' were scattered remnants of broken masonry, though a fine example of ancient wrought iron-work gates was to be found hanging in one of the gaps. Behind these lay a sprawling collection of once-imposing buildings.

When they reached the town, they asked one or two passers-by for directions to an inn. One answered in the ancient—and incomprehensible—language of academics. Another leaned back against a wall and stroked his chin, then after a pause, began, 'Well, it depends what you mean by "inn". In the time of King Thributhious the Great, an "inn" implied a den of iniquitous living where brawls and gambling were to be expected. But in more recent times the usage has become changed to a house for business transactions to be worked out while the participants eat together late into the night. Now, if you want somewhere to gamble . . .'

Rowanne and Gemma looked at each other in horror. 'No, thank you, we just want somewhere to stay the night and rest our horses.'

'Ah!' said the man, with a gleam in his eye, 'you're taking the definition as proposed by Theumious in his erudite essay . . .'

But they never heard the rest. Gently they nudged their mounts to move off and left the man expounding to himself.

All the buildings were fine, but very old and in a poor state of repair. Everywhere they looked, the people seemed preoccupied with nothing, or just stood on street corners talking. But most people looked well fed and dressed. The town seemed to be suffering from neglect more than poverty.

At last they turned a corner and saw an ancient, very low building with a door which sat at a slant in a skewed frame. Over the door hung the sign of a bush. An inn!

They knocked on the door and a short, fat woman answered it. She had flour up to her elbows and a friendly face. Here at last was someone who might be a little more use to them.

'Do you have a room for two, please?'

'Yes, yes, come in,' smiled the woman. But as Fleabag sprang down to follow them inside, the woman's foot shot out. 'But no cats! Especially black ones. Bad luck, go away, ugh, shoo!' and she spat at him.

Fleabag sat in the mud and stared up in amazement. Rowanne shrugged and made to go into the house, but Gemma shook her head. Taking Porridge's rein, she turned away. 'I'll call for you in the morning, Rowanne. We'll find somewhere else.'

Rowanne cast a regretful glance at the landlady and sniffed at the sweet smell of freshly baked bread emanating from her kitchen.

The woman was still threatening Fleabag with her broom. There would be no room for negotiation. There was nothing for it—Rowanne dared not leave Gemma on her own again. They would have to find somewhere else.

17

An Invitation to the Great Hall

Everywhere they went, there was the same reaction. At the signs of the Bull's Head, the Two Lanterns, the Dancing Bear: no cats in the house . . . especially black ones.

At last, at a small hostelry bearing the sign of the Bush of Broom, Fleabag rolled in some ash to make himself grey and slipped off round the back to hide in the stable with the horses.

At dinner that night, Rowanne overheard several students talking about the death of the Queen and the great quest for the Ring. From what they said, it sounded as if there had been many questers on the road, who were considered fair game to be told a great many tall tales, relieved of their purses and sent packing again. The lads seemed to think it was all good sport. 'If they only knew the truth . . . If they only *knew!*' spluttered one of the voices gleefully.

'A fool and his money are soon parted,' quipped another and raucous laughter filled the taproom.

Rowanne bought several pots of honey ale and

took the tray over to the students' table, asking if she could join them.

'I have been travelling for many months with my squire over there,' and she jerked a thumb at Gemma. 'We have only heard rumours of these happenings. What can you tell us that is true?'

One of the students, a gaunt-faced, narrow-eyed boy, looked hard at Rowanne and swallowed the honey ale in one gulp. Still staring hard, he wiped his mouth on his sleeve. 'More,' he demanded bluntly.

Rowanne ordered bread and cheese and more ale. Then, returning his stare, she sat astride the stool opposite him. 'Now,' she said. 'You were saying?'

The narrow-eyed lad licked his lips and began. 'There are stories of great magic and evil deeds. Only the Chancellor of All Wizards really knows of course. But it is said that the Queen was put into a trance and her Ring of Office was forced from her hand by that evil magician, the Fire Wielder. Then, by terrible spells which blackened the sky and froze the very blood of those who were near, the Fire itself was taken from the Ring. Until the two are brought together again, the land is in great peril.

'For,' he leaned forward and whispered, 'it is said the Fire cannot last without the Ring—or without some creature willing to let it live within it. But who could submit to such immense forces and live?

'Well, in Porthwain, we know that no human creature can carry the Fire without being consumed. The truth is that it is only his Holiness, the Chancellor of All Wizards, who keeps the Fire alive by spells . . .' and here he whispered even more quietly, ' . . . which are too terrible to speak of!'

At this the boy sat up and looked very pleased with himself. Rowanne glanced around to see if the other students were laughing . . . was it a huge joke they dished out to every traveller? But there was not the flicker of a smile on any face. They had all turned pale and wide-eyed with terror.

Gemma sat silently in the shadows, well away from the speakers. She pressed her hands closed under the table lest the burning feeling in her hands should burst out and flare up with all the beauty of the Ring Fire. Her cheeks were flushed with anger at the terrible lies the boy was telling. But she sat alone in rigid silence, hardly daring to breathe.

The boy was looking hopefully into the depths of his ale pot again.

Rowanne did not order more. Instead, she compelled the boy's gaze one more time. 'I don't believe a word of it,' she said slowly and deliberately.

Gemma gasped and bit her lip. There would be trouble now, for sure.

The boy did not react, except to raise one eyebrow. 'Oh? Then perhaps you ought to meet the Chancellor of All Wizards to see for yourself how ill he looks with the effort of holding all our great land together with his spells and his will. Then you would understand how he casts his gaze around to seek the whereabouts of the Ring so that peace and justice may be restored . . . For truly, the small riots and unrests we hear of will soon turn into war if this thing is not quickly resolved, one way or another.'

The boy glared piercingly under his thin lashes and pushed his drinking pot across the table.

Rowanne ordered more ale, but did not pour it. Instead she watched the candles flicker their pale light across the lad's face. The other students had pulled back as if they sensed things beyond their control.

'Yes,' said Rowanne carefully. 'Although I am a mere knight who has no knowledge of these things, perhaps I should meet his Holiness, the Chancellor of All Wizards.'

The boy tapped the jug with his drinking pot, but said nothing.

When the pot was full, he said: 'Tomorrow night, you will be invited to dine at nine o'clock, in the Great Hall of the university.' And with that he drained the honey ale and left the inn.

After a few seconds, his silent companions got up and followed him.

The room was left in a chilling silence.

At last Gemma said quietly, 'I'm going to bed.'

'You're daft!' announced Fleabag, perched on the wooden rail at the foot of Rowanne's bed. Gemma was busy washing away the dusty pawprints on the window ledge where the cat had got in.

'I don't need your advice, thank you!' announced Rowanne in a chilly tone. She was sitting on a stool in front of a mirror putting eye make-up on. 'When you've done that, I want you to do my hair, Gemma.'

'Don't you ever say "please"?' complained the cat. 'She's not your servant, you know.'

Rowanne was about to say, 'Of course she is,' but she bit her lip and just mumbled 'please', under her breath.

'Why are you going to all this trouble?' Gemma broke in, surprised at her own daring. 'You're dressed in your best silk gown and you've ordered a carriage . . . it's obvious that the man hasn't got the Ring. And the boy could have been spinning you a tale just to get drunk for free . . .'

Rowanne mixed her eye colours vigorously in their little pots. She was angry. 'But he knows *something*—and I intend to find out what. And it is easier to get what I want to know from a man if I dress like a courtier rather than a knight.'

'But he will be most suspicious about what a lady like you is doing here. The curious traveller was a far better disguise.'

Rowanne winced as Gemma tugged at a stray loop of hair which did not want to sit in its place on top of her head. 'I can hardly go to dinner dressed in my leather trousers and coat, can I? I don't even have my formal knightly gear with me. No, don't worry. I know what I'm doing.'

Just then, a maid knocked on the door. Fleabag shot under the bed and hid. 'Your carriage is here, Ma'am.' The girl stopped and peered at the end of Fleabag's tail which poked out from under the counterpane. 'Forgive me, Ma'am, but I think I left fluff under your bed. I'll get a brush immediately.'

'No, no,' said Gemma in a hurry. 'It's my furry slippers. They're rather old and disreputable, I'm afraid, but I'm very fond of them,' and with that she kicked the whole of Fleabag's backside right under the bed. 'Please don't bother to come back tonight, I'm going to bed early.'

'As you wish,' said the girl and left the room.

Gemma helped Rowanne on with her soft, white angora shawl and watched her walk elegantly out of the door.

Turning back into the room, Gemma went to the dresser and picked up the cream vellum invitation that had arrived that morning. 'To the Lady Knight at the Bush of Broom. His Holiness the Chancellor of All Wizards requests the pleasure of your company for dinner tonight at the University Great Hall.'

'Perhaps she's right,' sighed Gemma. 'She would have looked out of place dressed in travelling clothes at a formal dinner. But I wish she hadn't gone. I have a bad feeling about this Chancellor. What do you think, Fleabag?'

But there was no answer.

Gemma knelt down and peered under the bed. Was he sulking because she'd described him as a 'disreputable old slipper'? Nothing there, except a trail of ash and a half-eaten mouse. Really, he could have had his snack outside. She picked the poor thing up by what was left of its tail and threw it out of the window.

Fleabag, meanwhile, had slipped out of the back door while Rowanne was being helped into the carriage (she was never much good at doing anything when she had a skirt on). He had skilfully hidden behind her silks and crouched under the carriage seat, so stealthily that even Rowanne did not know he was there.

At the Great Hall, a footman stepped forward and opened the carriage door.

'I am the Lady Knight Rowanne de Montiland,' she announced, 'I have an invitation to dine with his Holiness the Chancellor of All Wizards.'

The footman bowed obsequiously and helped her down.

She was led up great white marble steps that fanned in a wide semi-circle from a piazza up to a huge, pillared front entrance. At the top of the steps, enormous carved oak doors stood open, streaming golden light from candelabras onto the white stone. The footman led her through long corridors decorated with statues of great men and women of wisdom and learning. At last he stopped outside another massive set of doors and bowed again.

'The Lady Knight Rowanne de Montiland,' he announced pompously. As Rowanne stepped inside the room, the doors were shut behind her with a dull thud.

Left alone outside, Fleabag said something very rude in rat language. He had sprung from statue to statue, keeping well out of sight all the way up the corridor, but this last and trickiest manoeuvre of getting into the room with Rowanne had not worked.

He sat in the cobwebby recesses of the plinth that held the bust of one of the previous chancellors—a cross-looking old woman—and washed himself thoroughly.

'She's mad,' he said to himself over and over again. 'I can smell only trouble ahead. And what's worse, she's given her full name and title. Even kittens know that you never give your full name and title to a *wizard*—it only makes it easier for them to work spells on you.'

Once he had cleaned the ash from his fur well enough for it to stop itching, Fleabag curled up for a catnap. To get that stupid woman out of this was going to need brainpower, and that required sleep.

His Holiness the Chancellor of all Wizards was tall, slim and elegant. He had neither the white whiskers nor the pointed hat that Rowanne had half expected. Like all the people from the West, he was fair and broad-boned, and his beard and hair were immaculately cut. He was dressed in a vermilion silk robe, embroidered with gold and yellow flames from the floor-sweeping hem to the superbly cut collar at his throat.

He stood quite still in the centre of a round room. The walls were plain white stone with windows set up high, meeting to make a glass lantern roof.

With a pang in the pit of her stomach, Rowanne realized that he was dressed in a garb to copy the true Fire Wielder and that the room was a copy of the Hall of Light.

She curtseyed, as she felt it was expected. At this, the Chancellor's face lost its suave rigidity and loosened into a smile. 'My dear,' he said, in tones smooth as honey, 'welcome.'

He stepped forward and took her hand to kiss it.

As he bowed over her fingers, he glanced up at her with ice-pale eyes to enjoy the look of shock on her face, when she realized that his hand bore a huge, plain ring set with an opal—an opal with no fire at its heart.

18

Dining on Spells

Still holding her hand, the Chancellor led her to a table in the very centre of the room. It was laid for a formal meal for two, set with cut crystal glasses and exquisitely fine bone china plates.

With perfect courtesy, the Chancellor helped Rowanne to her seat. Another, smaller door opened and a tall, thin young man entered, dressed in a grey silk tunic and trousers. He bowed and kissed Rowanne's hand. As he stood, she knew she recognized him, but could not remember where she had seen him before.

'Allow me to present my son, Sethan.'

Sensing Rowanne's hesitation, the Chancellor continued, 'It was he, of course, whom you met at the Bush of Broom last night. He was so impressed by your generous hospitality to a poor student that he begged to be allowed to return the honour tonight. He will be waiting on us.'

Rowanne tried to murmur something about buying the lad a drink being a pleasure, but a sweet-scented clear white wine was already being poured and Sethan was organizing servants, approaching with trays of exquisite delicacies.

The courses came constantly, dish after dish. Rowanne was coaxed to taste everything. Each was accompanied by a different wine or cordial, all of which she was urged at least to sip.

Slowly, Rowanne became aware that she was unsure of the conversation. The Chancellor seemed to be doing most of the talking—mostly anecdotes about his time as a student and how hard it had been. He moved on to his rise to Chancellorship, how he had struggled against all opposition to prove himself worthy of the position. Then he started to talk about how it had been shown to him by various divinations that still greater things were within his grasp.

He told her that he had acquired the ring—he did not say how—to help him achieve this greatness for which he had been born.

'You see, my dear,' he smiled and patted her hand as Sethan passed a silver dish of fresh truffles for her to try, 'I am destined to be the next Fire Wielder. But unlike the others, with my mystical powers, I will reign for ever.'

Rowanne screwed up her eyes to try to see his face clearly, but it was swimming in and out of her vision. One second it was huge and lowering over her; the next moment he seemed almost to have disappeared.

She must excuse herself. She had to get some air and clear her head . . .

But try as she might, she could not move, and he was still talking. 'Very soon, my dear, something wonderful is going to happen. As you know, in the past, a king or a queen needed a Fire Wielder to reign with him or her, but . . .' (here his face began to swim across the ceiling until Rowanne had to crane her neck right back to see. If only she could get out . . .)

' . . . but I will be both. I will be the perfect ruler. Complete in myself.' He pressed his fingertips together and smiled benignly.

Rowanne found herself struggling to say something, but she could not move. Her limbs had become as heavy as lead.

Sethan lifted one more wine glass to her lips with encouraging words to try this, the finest wine from his father's cellar. Rowanne did not want to drink it. She was already so dazed she felt she was slipping away to somewhere she did not want to go. But as soon as the glass was set to her lips, she drank as thirstily as if she had just crossed the Southern Desert.

Everything in her head seemed to shrink, until she was only aware of the tiny point of one candle flame.

The Chancellor slipped the opal ring from his finger and held it to reflect the flame so the fire seemed to burn from within it. Rowanne gasped and began to shake, her eyes staring wildly.

The Chancellor nodded to his son. 'She's ready,' he said. 'Help me carry her.' Rowanne was laid gently onto a *chaise longue* that had been hidden in the shadows. Servants removed the dining table and the bed was dragged into the very centre of the room. The opal ring was put on a little stand so Rowanne could see it, with the bright flame glinting through it.

The Chancellor drew up a chair and sat beside Rowanne. 'You will answer all my questions, Lady Knight Rowanne de Montiland. You will answer the truth completely and utterly.'

'I will,' she replied. Somewhere, deep in herself, a tiny part still struggled and screamed, but that soon faded to oblivion. There was nothing she could do to fight the drugs and magic that bound her. She was alone and trapped and there was no good sword within her hand's grasp. Not that she could have used it.

'What are you doing here?' asked the Chancellor.

'I am searching for the Queen's Ring.'

'Is this the Queen's Ring?'

'I do not know,' Rowanne replied dully.

'Who is with you?'

'A girl and a cat.'

At the sound of the word 'cat' two things happened. Firstly, Fleabag woke from his doze and realized it was time to take his favourite advice and do some eavesdropping and secondly, the Chancellor faltered and went pale.

'Where is the cat now?'

'I don't know. He was at the Bush of Broom, but he goes his own way. He turns up when he feels like it.'

'What is the cat's name?'

'Fleabag.'

'Is that all?'

'Yes.'

Fleabag smiled in his whiskers, glad that no one alive knew his real name. Only the Queen had known that, so no spells could be put on him very easily—as long as he did not eat or drink in this place.

The Chancellor said quietly to his son, 'As long as the cat is not black, we have nothing to fear. I am sure the time of our downfall cannot be yet. The prophecy spoke of times of glory before the end . . .'

Then he turned back to Rowanne. 'Who is the girl? What is her name?'

'She is known as Gemma Streetchild. She is a guttersnipe. She travels with me and acts as my maid.'

'Of no importance, father,' said the boy. 'I saw her last night. She was a scared child who sat in the corner and shook at the very sight of me. I am certain she cannot possibly be the Fire Maiden of whom we were warned.'

Again Fleabag sighed with relief. Gemma had never known her real name. 'Streetchild' was a nickname given to her at the palace.

'What do you know about the Ring?' the Chancellor persisted.

Mechanically and with a dull voice, Rowanne told all she knew about the Ring and about the taking of the Fire.

'Why did you come here to look for it?'

Fleabag held his breath. What would she say? Would she explain about Gemma hearing the Ring Fire speak? At the moment the Chancellor was asking all the wrong questions to get the truth from Rowanne. As long as he kept off tack, all might yet be well.

'I came here because it seemed to me that if the Ring is not kept in the houses of royalty, then it must be resting in the halls of wisdom.'

'Why did you come here tonight?'

'Because the boy in the inn made me suspect that the Chancellor might know something to help me find the Ring.'

'By the Quenching of the Fire! She doesn't know!' The boy stamped in fury and frustration.

'I'm not so sure. I think the truth drug is fading. Her mind is bound with strong spells which will hold, but we will not get much further tonight. More of the truth drug might kill her and I don't want that yet. Not until I've drained her of what she knows, and I'm sure she knows *something*.

'I have just not touched on the right trigger question. What have I missed?' The Chancellor paced up and down the circular chamber, stroking his well-trimmed beard. For several minutes the swish of his silken robes was the only sound.

'Father,' said the boy at last. 'She has fallen asleep.'

The man strode over to Rowanne and lifted one of her eyelids. He clicked his fingers a few times, but there was no response. He sighed. 'That's it for tonight. I cannot help but feel we are terribly close to the answer . . .

'In the morning I must supervise the Convocation of the Wise. I may be able to slip away in the afternoon . . .'

Then he smiled. 'No. What I will do is to cancel the dinner with the professors of philosophy in the evening. They will be so busy worrying about what is meant by "dinner" they won't notice anyway. During the day, make sure she is comfortable. She will only sleep, I am sure. At dusk I will say the spell that will enable me to take her mind from her into my own.

'We can arrange for her body to be found dead at the bottom of a wall or something. There won't be any problem there. Take her away and get some sleep, boy. Tomorrow will be a long day.'

Fleabag soon found a way out of the Hall. Doors had been left open all over the place. Although the kitchen rubbish bin looked most tempting, he could not risk eating anything in case it was magic or drugged.

First he must get back to Gemma with a report of what had happened. Because he had travelled blindly beneath a carriage seat, he had not been able to see or smell the route, so it was almost dawn before he found the Bush of Broom. All the doors were locked, and Gemma's window was fastened against the night's chilly wind. There was nothing to do except curl up in the stable. But even deep in the warm straw, he could not sleep. Finally he went out again.

Gemma did not sleep well either. She had expected Rowanne back late, but somewhere at the back of her mind, she knew that the knight had not come in at all. She woke, stiff and unrefreshed, and went to the pump in the yard to fetch herself some water—she never saw much point in waiting for a maid to do what she could perfectly well do for herself.

Once again she shivered with the strange notion that she was being watched. She had not felt it for a long time—not since Rowanne had found her ill in the shepherd's hut. She told herself not to be so silly, and the feeling went with the first splash of icy water on her skin. She fed the horses and kicked Fleabag awake with a friendly toe under his black pelt.

But it didn't feel like Fleabag.

She looked closer. It was a human head, hidden under the straw. For a second, she hesitated. Should she call the innkeeper? What if it was someone on the run? Her hands tingled just a little as she pushed the straw aside. The person was lying very still, perhaps pretending to be dead? It was a man... would he pounce? She stepped back and grabbed a pitchfork. Then she called as quietly and as steadily as she could, 'Stand up. I want to talk to you. If you do as you are told, I will not hurt you.'

The figure slowly stood on his feet and risked looking at his captor.

'Phelan?' she whispered, lowering the pitchfork. 'What are you doing here skulking like a thief?'

He grinned, showing his strong white teeth. 'I *am* a thief, in case you'd forgotten.'

At that second, Fleabag sprang into the stable, wet, cold and in such a panic he made the horses start. Phelan turned and quietened them with a sure hand.

'Quick, quick,' howled the cat. 'Grab what you can and get out of here. The whole town will be after us soon.'

'I know which horses are yours,' Phelan said. 'I'll get them saddled, you pack what you can. I'll meet you in the courtyard.'

'If I value my fur I must get out unseen!' Fleabag wailed.

Gemma had never seen the cat really ruffled before.

'Come with me,' she said, 'I'll pack you in the luggage.' With that, she scooped him up and carried him in under her towel.

Inside the room, Gemma flung clothes into their bags, while Fleabag stalked the room uneasily, recounting the night's adventures in the Great Hall of the university.

'. . . I got back here at dawn, but couldn't sleep. I knew Phelan had been following us for some time, so I went and found him and told him we really needed his help. I had hoped to get back here in time to warn you, but you know this place has a thing about black cats?'

Gemma nodded as she pushed Rowanne's riding boots into the recesses of her bag.

'Well, I gathered last night that there is some sort of prophecy that a Fire Maiden and a black cat will be the downfall of this particularly evil Chancellor.

'I couldn't resist it, could I? It was too good a joke to miss. I simply had to give them all a scare and have some fun. So as soon as it was really light I went back and I climbed the roof of the Great Hall. I started parading around with my tail in the air, declaring at the top of my voice the imminent demise of the Chancellor and his followers.

'You would never believe the commotion I caused. I'd have kept my whiskers and tail to myself if only I'd known what the result would be . . . I soon had archers shooting at me, wizards chanting at me and lawyers yelling legal clauses—(though my clawses were better than theirs!)—everyone telling me not to be a bad puss and to come down.

'At first I just laughed at them but then they set the dogs on me . . . not just nice little lap doggies like the ones at the palace—you know, the sort you say 'meow' to and they turn pale and run. No. These were *proper* dogs.'

He stopped talking and cocked an ear. 'And I think I can hear them a few streets away. Is that Rowanne's perfume? Good, smother me in it so I don't smell of cat quite so clearly.

'I got away by jumping into a pond at the back of the library. The dogs lost the scent completely, then I crept round the outside of the city. Oh, I thought I would never see you again!' and he jumped up and gave her a big lick on the nose.

'No time for being daft,' she laughed as she pushed him down on top of a load of dirty washing she had meant to tackle that morning. 'This lot will help to cover your cat smell, too.'

'Pooh!' said Fleabag from under the leather bag flap. 'I see what you mean.'

'Shut UP!' she warned him, pushing him down. 'And whatever happens, lie still.' She snatched at Rowanne's purse, left some coins on the table for payment, swung the bags over her shoulders and went out into the courtyard.

Phelan was there already with the horses bridled and saddled.

He looked at her roughly cut hair and squire's clothes, then handed her a dollop of mud. 'Dirty yourself and keep mum. I'll do the talking.' He mounted a horse lightly and trotted out into the street.

The sounds of dogs howling on leashes could be clearly heard only a few streets away. They obviously had a cat in their sights. There were plenty of the animals, even in Porthwain, but was this a black one? Gemma hoped not.

19

Fire Maiden

The town did not have a proper garrison. A few raggle-taggle soldiers kept some sort of order, but they were not trained like Rupert's men, or the Queen's Guard.

A thick-set, fair woman, dressed in the university colours of dark and light blue, challenged the fugitives with a raised sword. Even Gemma could see that she did not know how to use it.

'Halt!' she demanded. 'Who goes there?'

'Cough loudly,' Phelan whispered. 'And keep coughing.'

Phelan put on a thick Southern accent. ' 'Tis only a poor man from the South, Phelan Muckraker and his brother Gorthrod. We have been to see the good doctors of this town, but they cannot cure him . . .'

At this point Gemma coughed until she felt her lungs would burst.

Phelan leaned across the horse's neck and made sure he spat when he spoke. ' 'Tis sad, my brother seems to have the plague and . . .'

But he could not finish his sentence. The woman stepped back and wiped the spit from her face as she screamed, 'Plague! Plague! Get them out! Plague!'

Gemma buried her head because she could not stop giggling. She hoped her convulsive shaking would be taken for fever instead of uncontrolled laughter. Several passers-by hit the horses with sticks to make them run faster. Galloping wildly they fled past the massive dogs who strained at their leashes, but the cry of 'plague' had gone before and the dogs were pulled back.

In the depths of his saddle-bag, Fleabag chuckled as he heard the dogs howling to their masters that there was a cat with the horses. But the masters were either too stupid to understand the dog-speech, or too frightened of the plague to do anything. Within minutes, Phelan, Gemma and Fleabag were riding free as birds down the hill and away from the town.

At the first wood they came to, they pulled rein and stopped to water the animals. The horses had a few cuts where they had been beaten with sticks, but nothing too bad.

Fleabag climbed out of his prison and rolled on the grass to rid himself of the stink of perfume and dirty clothes.

'Clever Phelan. That was almost worthy of a cat's wit!'

Phelan grinned and bowed. 'Sir Cat, I am honoured.'

Gemma clambered down and faced the boy. 'What are you doing here, Phelan? It's not that I'm not pleased to see you, but where did you spring from? And how did you know which horses were ours?'

Phelan grinned 'I was worried when you left

Rupertsberg. I wanted to go with you, but—well, I am only a common thief, fit for the scaffold and you are on the Queen's business. You have had dealings with the Ring Fire . . . As I said, I would put it out as soon as look at it!'

Gemma shook her head, 'But . . .'

Fleabag put up a paw. 'Let him finish,' he said. 'We'll talk about things being right and wrong later.'

'Well, I followed you. I must have missed you somewhere, for I lost you for several days. I guessed you might be heading for Porthwain and I had some luck with a lift on a farm cart. I thought I had lost you completely until I saw you arriving two days ago. I met up with old Fleabag in the market yesterday and he told me everything you've been up to. He said he had a feeling you might need me, so I wasn't surprised when he came and got me this morning.'

'I'm glad you did.' Gemma smiled, stroking the cat. 'I couldn't bear to think of my best friend as dog-meat.'

Fleabag shivered. 'Don't say such things please, even in jest!'

'At least it explains the horrid feeling I've had for ages that we were being followed. I just wish you'd told me who it was, you wretched cat. I've been really quite scared at times.'

'You never asked,' replied Fleabag coolly as he began to wash.

Gemma took a low swipe at him but turned it into a scratch behind his left ear. 'I forgive you, this time,' she laughed. 'But now we are sitting still for a few moments, you must tell Phelan what happened to Rowanne.'

Fleabag stopped washing and, for once, cracked no jokes.

When the story was told, Gemma bit her lip. 'I had a feeling she was walking into something dangerous, but she wouldn't listen. The only question now is, how are we going to get her out? Facing danger is one thing, but surely we would need the Fire Wielder himself to stand up to the Chancellor?'

'Are you sure you *want* to rescue her?' Fleabag muttered, rolling onto his back and letting the wintry sun warm his tummy.

'Of *course* we are going to rescue her!' replied Gemma indignantly. 'She may be a cat-hater, but she was sent on this quest too... by the Fire Wielder no less.' She paused. 'But what frightens me most is that if the Chancellor of All Wizards says the spell to take Rowanne's mind from her, then he will know everything she knows. Then he may follow us and we may lead him to the Ring. We must rescue her to protect the quest, if for no other reason.'

'True,' mused the cat in his upside-downy voice, as he scratched at a wandering flea. 'But don't you think everything would be easier without her?'

'No!' replied Gemma firmly. 'Bother it, we need her!'

Fleabag wriggled hard, rubbing his back on the fallen pine cones. He had a look of intense concentration on his face. But he could not stay serious for long. At last he chuckled, 'You win! I was only teasing. We'll rescue that cat-hater, but I beg you, never tell any of my relatives what I'm about to do, or I'll be called a poodle for the rest of my days.'

'I am glad,' Gemma said mischievously. 'If Rowanne wasn't with us you'd have to annoy me instead. I don't think I could face that.'

'Mind you,' Fleabag added, 'if she threatens me one more time after this, I'm off. You can come with me if you like, but a cat can only take so much . . . Now, let me get some sleep so I can think.'

No one spoke for a while. They sat wrapped in blankets listening to the wind rattling the bare branches of the trees.

The clouds grew thick and heavy early in the afternoon, making it almost dark. Phelan found shelter for the horses in a dip in the ground, more or less out of the wind. The cat snoozed in one of the saddle-bags. Phelan lit a small fire and they huddled in blankets while a rabbit roasted.

'Why did you run away at the hostel?' Gemma asked. 'You didn't even say goodbye.'

Phelan shrugged. 'Why should you want me to? My friends and I tried to kill you. I was the cause of your arguing with the Lady Rowanne and not sleeping in luxury in the palace. I had done you nothing but harm. Anyway, being caught in my company is no great honour. If I'd been recognized and put in prison, they might have taken you as well. As I told you before, Prince Rupert has no great reputation for justice.'

'I was lonely when you went. Oh, I know I've got Fleabag, but he's not always there and I need as many friends as I can get.'

'Why do you stick with the Lady Rowanne?'

'Well, she may be difficult, but we were told to help each other. We've just got to find a way of getting on together if possible. Anyway, in an odd sort of a way I'll miss her and—and we can't just let her die. That's just not the right way to do things, is it? It's just like we couldn't let you die. For the moment at least, we belong together. And she has been quite nice to me lately.'

Phelan pulled the blankets closer. The day was getting colder and he could sense the night would be worse. 'For what it's worth, I'll help in whatever way I can. Now look, I don't know what sort of idea that fur-brained cat of yours comes up with. We'd better know what we're going to do if—I mean when we escape. We won't be out of the town until after dark and I think I can smell snow in the air. We'll need to have somewhere we can run straight to and be able to rest. Especially if anyone gets injured.'

Gemma climbed to the lip of the hollow and surveyed the countryside beyond the wood. 'There are farmhouses with barns and sheds further along the road. But a lot depends on how fit Rowanne is. If she can ride we'll make it, but if there's a hue and cry after us or if she's still unconscious, we'll need somewhere closer to hand. Here's as good a place as any, I suppose,' she added, shivering.

'It's going to be a chilly night, I think,' said Phelan.

'I'm freezing already, and I can smell perfectly good rabbit burning,' moaned Fleabag as he jumped down to the ground, stretching his back, tail and all three paws.

'Now,' said Fleabag, his mouth full of food. 'As I told you this morning, there seems to be some sort of prophecy about a Fire Maiden and a black cat which terrifies the wits out of this Chancellor. I pushed my luck a bit this morning, by acting the black cat part, but what I really needed was a Fire Maiden with me. So what we will do is this . . .'

Phelan left the horses in a small side-alley near the Great Hall. They were good animals and he knew they would come when he whistled.

As there were few guards of any sort, they managed to reach the main door before they were challenged. Gemma held herself tall and tried to imitate Rowanne's 'imperious' voice. 'I have had a dream. I need to speak to the Chancellor immediately. There is great danger for him at the very door of his house.'

The guard bowed and swiftly led the young woman and her attendant to the doors of the small round chamber.

'You may leave us!' said Gemma, waving her hand dismissively.

The guard looked surprised but obeyed. As soon as he was out of sight, Phelan opened the satchel on his shoulder and let Fleabag jump down to the floor. Gemma then threw her cloak back to show the flame-red silk dress she had borrowed from Rowanne's baggage. Phelan lit the two large torches that Gemma had smuggled in under her cloak, and knocked on the door.

There was no answer, but low voices could be heard within. With heart pounding Phelan threw the doors open and announced, 'The Fire Maiden has come with her black cat to claim your life. Tremble and fear!'

147

At first the Chancellor threw back his head and laughed scornfully. 'Don't be silly children,' he snapped. 'Go away, I am busy. Go and play your games somewhere else.' But Gemma did not move. Fleabag jumped up on the table where a great book of illuminated texts lay open with phials and plants neatly arranged next to it.

Meanwhile Gemma could hear Phelan stealthily making his way around the room to reach Rowanne lying on her couch in the shadows. Once he had managed to get her out, all they had to do was run . . . *all* they had to do! She could feel the fear tightening in her chest and the noise of blood pounded deafeningly in her ears.

Abruptly the Chancellor stopped laughing. He took a swipe at Fleabag with a stone pestle. But his erratic movement missed the cat and sent some of the glass phials crashing to the floor.

Sethan sprang forward and grabbed Fleabag, who twisted in the boy's grasp and scratched his face and eyes again and again, until blood flowed profusely. In agony he dropped the cat who sprang back to the table and faced his foe, spitting hideously.

But the Chancellor seemed to be ignoring everything. He was intent on making signs in chalk on the floor and chanting an ugly-sounding rhyme.

'How . . . how did you get in here?' sobbed Sethan, nursing his face.

'There were hardly any guards,' replied the cat.

'But we don't need them. The place is ringed with magic. Only the Ring Fire itself could get past the spells we have placed . . .'

'Shut up!' yelled his father. 'A spell must have slipped somewhere. Probably one *you* made. I'm always telling you to be more careful. It *must* be your fault. The Ring Fire could not come this far north without me knowing. The Fire Wielder's every step is watched and reported to me daily. At this very moment he is asleep in the palace at Harflorum.'

With that the Chancellor lifted his arms high and began to chant out loud.

'Watch out!' yelled Fleabag, as bright blue flame sprung from the chalk lines and surrounded the Chancellor. From the centre of it came an arc of greenish light that reached out for Gemma.

The girl was too scared to move. She just held onto her torches and thought very hard of the day the Fire Wielder placed a little Fire into her palms.

'I won't forget,' she whispered. 'I won't forget!'

As she did so, the green light faded, but the blue flames around the Chancellor rose even higher.

Again he threw an arc of light, but this time it was purple. Again Gemma thought of the Fire in her hands and again the purple light faded.

Drawing all his strength and power to himself, the Chancellor summoned lightning from the sky.

This time Gemma was so terrified, she dropped her torches and grabbed the big book from the table to hold over her head.

With an immense crack of thunder, the lightning hit the book, setting it alight.

'Not my precious book!' screamed the Chancellor, jumping through the flames to grab it back. But as he did so, the long trailing skirts of his robe caught in the blue flames and he fell to the floor, screaming.

Sethan rushed to his side, but he too was caught in the hungry pool of cerulean heat.

Gemma could not bear the sight of their agony. She had not meant to hurt anyone. She reached out to help them, but both father and son cowered back at the sight of her. 'Not the Ring Fire! Take it away, the sight burns us . . .'

By this time the chamber was filled with attendants bearing water and fire brooms. But no one could get near the raging blue flames which roared and towered high above them until they licked the glass lantern roof.

'Run!' yelled Phelan. 'The whole place will be alight soon. We can do nothing.'

Rowanne was draped across his left shoulder, so Gemma took her other arm and between them they dragged her out of the room and along the corridor.

In the smoke and confusion, no one noticed them leaving. Fleabag soon appeared by their side and the four of them ran out into the night.

20

A Cottage in the Rocks

Everything was in turmoil when the three shadowy figures and the cat reached the flight of stairs down from the Great Hall to the piazza below. Snow was falling, making the steps slippery. Hundreds of people were pushing and shoving—some trying to get inside with pails of water, others fleeing the burning building in panic.

The four were buffeted and trampled. Gemma and Phelan dragged the all but lifeless Rowanne between them while the cat went ahead to bite the ankles of any who got in the way. The hubbub was so great that Phelan's piercing whistle could not be heard by the waiting horses and slowly the roar of the flames behind them was coming closer.

'Wait here,' called Fleabag as he dashed between the thundering, crushing feet, risking life and paw to reach the little alley where the horses stood quietly.

With one leap, he gained the mare's saddle. Try as he might, he could not whistle, but he managed to cajole and bully the two ponies into following. They had to pick their way gingerly through the seething confusion, but it did not take long to reach the steps of the Hall where Phelan and Gemma were framed against the flames and smoke. Behind them masonry was beginning to crash down.

A kindly man helped to heave Rowanne onto the back of one of the ponies.

When he saw Fleabag seated grimly on the back of the horse with Gemma behind him, the gold of the flames reflected in their wide eyes, he looked from one to another in amazement and shook his head. 'So it is true: the black cat and the Fire Maiden have come at last. All speed to you!'

Phelan took the rein of the pony carrying Rowanne. Carefully they eased their way through the team of fire-fighters and made for the north road.

The snow was falling faster as they left the noise and flames behind them. Fleabag jumped down and led the way down to the little hollow where they had camped earlier. Dismounting, Phelan coaxed the banked fire into life again, and they made camp as best they could. But it was a long, cold night.

At first light they struck camp. The snow had stopped, leaving only a light sprinkling, but the sky was still lowering blackly. Gemma wanted to get on the road again as quickly as possible.

But there was something she had to do first.

'Phelan, I want you to believe me when I say this. We all need you. I know what you have been, but that doesn't make you too bad to be a friend. Please don't disappear again. Without you, I won't get to wherever I'm supposed to be going. I can't look after Rowanne without help—she needs you too. And Fleabag needs someone to insult. Say you'll stay with us?'

Phelan was inspecting the ground and kicking at

the snow with the worn toes of his shoes. He was quiet for a few moments. 'Very well, just until the Lady is well enough to look after you all ... and to make sure she's not going to desert you again. I'll not stand for that a second time. But I'll have nothing to do with the search for the Ring if you don't mind. All that sort of thing makes me ... feel ill.'

Gemma nodded. 'I can't pretend I understand, but I'm grateful.'

Phelan helped Gemma heave Rowanne over the back of Pudding, the fat little pack pony, then he mounted the mare and took Pudding's rein. Gemma was glad to be back with Porridge again. Fleabag chose to walk. He said he wanted the exercise.

'What we need to do first,' suggested Gemma, 'is get back on the main road north by north-west. I should have realized things would go wrong when I heard Porthwain was slightly out of the way.'

They rode with the watery sun at their backs for several days. The winds became increasingly bitter, but the snow turned into icy, cutting sleet. Slowly the ground rose ahead of them into the foothills of the Gwithennick Mountains which lay solidly across the path as far as the eye could see, from the north-west to the north-east.

One miserable morning they were camping in a barn which was about as waterproof as a net curtain. Gemma was trying to make Rowanne drink a little, when Fleabag came and sat in front of the pile of spitting damp sticks that passed for a fire.

'It's no good. I hate having wet fur. We have to stop somewhere warm for the winter.'

Phelan was sorting wood, looking for something that might be burnable. He stopped and looked out of the door at the terrain. 'I've never seen mountains before. What are they like in winter? Are they warmer than here?'

Fleabag shivered and shook his pelt. 'No. Worse. Much worse.'

'Then my vote is with Fleabag. We need to stop to get Rowanne better if nothing else . . . and with all due respect to Gemma, I think you have to sit and think about what you are doing. Hearing voices that tell you to go north by north-west sounds a bit potty, if you don't mind my saying so. It doesn't mean it's not true, but you need a practical plan as well. Rest, warmth and food will help.'

Phelan stamped on a dry branch and it snapped with a loud noise. Gemma jumped, but Rowanne did not so much as flicker an eyelid. She was not improving.

For the first time, Gemma began to question why she was on this strange journey at all. In the beginning, while the memory of the Queen and her loving care were so fresh in Gemma's mind, everything had been simple. She had obeyed without question. But now it seemed so long ago—and as Phelan said, it sounded a bit daft.

But if her quest was real, dare she stop? They had wasted valuable weeks at Rupertsberg. Since Rowanne had become caught in the Chancellor's spells at Porthwain they had been travelling painfully slowly. Already it was early November, and the year and a day was slipping away. If they rested for the winter months it would mean they would have to turn back as soon as the snow melted—having found nothing.

Here they were, at the foot of the Gwithennick Mountains. Snow would block the north by north-west road before they could reach the mountain passes. They could neither go on nor go back. She looked at the others. She owed it to them to rest—and to think.

She nodded. 'I agree,' she said. 'But where shall we go?'

Phelan stood up and sheltered his eyes against the cutting winds. He peered all around. 'What do you fancy? A farm where we can beg work for the winter and earn our keep, or a place of our own?'

Gemma looked worried.

'The farms around here are terribly poor and run-down,' Phelan continued. 'They are all owned by the University and it seems nothing has been done to maintain them for years. I don't think we'd find anywhere which could afford to keep us for the winter—however hard we work.'

'Then it must be a place of our own,' Fleabag said decisively.

Phelan put down the branch he was breaking. 'If you will lend me the horse for the day, I will ride ahead and see what I can find. You might as well rest here. It's as good a place as any.' He looked at the huddled group and felt sorry for them. Everyone was so cold and wet.

'Take her,' said Gemma. 'But try and be back by nightfall, or we'll worry.'

Phelan brushed himself down and saddled the mare. Gemma handed him a thick blanket and some food. He turned the horse's head to the road and shivered. Everywhere looked so grey and miserable. The trees were bare and more rain was coming. These days the sky seemed to be perpetually weeping. Squeezing the horse's flanks with his heels, Phelan urged her into a trot and set off.

'You know what Rowanne would say, don't you?' said Fleabag unhappily.

'What?'

' "You'll never see that horse or that boy again. He'll ride away, sell it and go his own way." '

'Do you believe that?'

'No. Do you?'

Gemma shook her head. 'No. I always get a fierce burning feeling in my hands when something's wrong. I don't get that with him.' She poked at the fire and wished she had left it alone, for the charred twigs fell apart and the flames went out.

'I wish you could do something useful with your burning hands like light us a real fire,' moaned Fleabag.

'That'll be the day. But it would be nice, wouldn't it?'

The hours dragged on in their grey, damp unhappy way. In the early afternoon Gemma took the ponies for a run to warm them up a bit. As she returned, she saw a rider in the distance, coming in their direction very fast.

As the heavy thud of hooves approached they began to slow, as the horse was eased to a standstill.

Phelan swung down to the ground and ran down the little slope to the derelict barn.

'I've found just the place!' he proclaimed breathlessly. 'It's a bit tumbledown, but it's perfect. It's a deserted goatherd's hut in a small cleft, sheltered from the wind. If we hurry, we'll just get there by nightfall!'

Taking a cloth from his saddle bag, he rubbed the mare down and gave her a handful of bran. Then he helped the others pack. Heaving Rowanne up and across Pudding's saddle was a struggle and she had to be tied into place. At last the mare was cool enough to have a drink, after which they set off as fast as they could.

The weather held dry for them. A biting wind cut across the barren landscape and seemed to want to drive them back from the foothills. As they went on, sharp rises of rocky outcrops suddenly dipped into marshy flats, then rose steeply again. But the road was fairly good and kept north by north-west, much to Gemma's relief.

A few crofters' cottages were dotted across the landscape. Skinny, chilled-looking cattle and sheep huddled in the lee of anything which afforded shelter. As the light began to fail, Gemma became increasingly worried. The road was rising well above the plain now and the rocks were becoming slippery with evening ice. There were no buildings at all within sight.

Phelan caught the expression on her face and gave her a hearty slap on the back.

'Not far now. Look!' He pointed ahead to where the road seemed to detour around a rockfall. There was still no sign of a dwelling of any kind. Gemma bent her head doggedly to go on, patting Porridge's neck and talking gently to her. The pony was very tired.

Secretly, Gemma was beginning to wonder whether they had missed the cottage in the evening shadows.

Suddenly Phelan gave a whoop of delight and sprang to the ground. He led the mare away from the road and across a short grassy slope. Then he disappeared. 'We're here!' he yelled triumphantly. 'Come on!'

Fleabag jumped down from Pudding, where he had been curled up on Rowanne's back to help keep her warm. The pony followed the cat and Gemma came next leading the tired, patient Porridge.

The cottage was certainly 'a bit tumbledown'. It had been invisible from the road because it was little more than a roof across a wide split in a rock. The front was built of dry-stone walling with a wooden door. But as Phelan had said, it was at least better shelter than they had been used to.

The cottage was roughly triangular. The door to the first room was still more or less on its hinges, but had little roof left. It was big enough to shelter the ponies from the wind. Behind this, a second, smaller room was built deep into the rock. It was very dark, but dry and just about big enough to let everyone lie down comfortably.

Phelan managed to get a small fire going. Bread and water were passed round and, for the first time in over a week, everyone was warm.

Soon Phelan and Fleabag were asleep, but Gemma's night was disturbed by dreams. They were not unpleasant. In fact they reminded her of something far off—something, some time which had been good. They seemed to be echoes of the things she used to see when she watched the Fire in the Queen's Ring.

When she woke, she found her hands were burning more fiercely than ever.

Carefully she climbed across Rowanne and went to build up the fire, which was slowly falling to ash.

She sat staring into the flames until dawn. Phelan was right. What was she doing on this quest? Did she only *wish* the Queen had sent her? What possible use could she be to anyone? What did she know about the Ring or the Fire?

As dawn began to lighten the corners of the little shelter. Phelan woke. 'Did you know you were thinking aloud?' he asked quietly, squatting down beside her.

Gemma hung her head. 'Sorry.'

Phelan laughed. 'Don't be. I didn't want to make you doubt what you are doing, I just felt you needed time to rest and think. With winter coming on, it seemed like a good time to stop.'

Gemma looked at him through hazy tears. 'But I don't *know* what I'm doing or where I'm going, or why. I don't know how anyone could ever hope to find the Ring in all this wide land. Rowanne might know some answers—but she's in this strange magic sleep. Ever since we left Porthwain I've been worried sick that we came too late and that the spell to take her mind from her has already been said. Are we just carrying the shell of Rowanne? Can we do anything?'

Phelan turned to look at the knight. She was very pale and breathing in a slow, shallow rhythm. He lifted her wrist and felt the throb of life in her veins.

'I don't know,' he said. 'I have some knowledge of herbs and fungi I picked up while living in the woods. I can try and rouse her. But I think it's going to need something stronger than potions to heal her.'

'You mean more magic?'

Phelan shook his head. 'No. Something stronger even than magic.'

He left Gemma looking wide eyed and worried as he got up to go and fetch water. He found Fleabag devouring a rather scrawny rat outside the door.

'Awful hunting around here,' he moaned. 'Couldn't you do better than this? I ordered the best hotel with room service and milk on a saucer every morning. I'm not paying for this!' he grumbled, 'I'm complaining to the management!'

Phelan paused and went back. He picked up the cat by the scruff of the neck and looked him in the eye. 'I bested you once, cat. I can best you again. Watch it!' he grinned, giving Fleabag a friendly cuff as he put him down gently.

Fleabag looked as sheepish as a cat can. 'Would you care for some rat's leg—or maybe a nice bit of ear? A bit chewy but very tasty—sir?'

21

Fungus Soup

For the first few days, they divided their time between repairing the cottage and looking for food. Fleabag caught some partridges and a hare and Phelan bought vegetables and hay from one of the nearby crofts.

Much of the roof-support timber was still usable. It just had to be pushed back into place and held firm with narrow wedges of stone. The roof itself they remade with flat fir branches covered with cut turfs. They twisted ropes from heather stems to lash the roof down and weighted it with small boulders.

There was plenty of dead wood for the fire and the cottage soon became warm and pleasant.

Everyone began to feel better—except Rowanne.

One day Phelan came back with a large piece of bark and a bag of toadstools. Banking up the fire so it smouldered rather than burned, he began to scrape some greenish-grey slime from the bark into the cooking pot. This he mixed with water and let simmer for several hours. He would not let Gemma cook the evening meal, as the fire had to be kept at a steady temperature and there was only one cooking pot.

Fleabag was not too bothered—he had caught a trout in a nearby river and was quite happy to eat it raw. Gemma chewed dried fruit and scowled.

'What are you doing? I'm famished, and that stuff stinks. I wouldn't eat it if I was dying of hunger.'

Phelan concentrated on stirring the pot. 'You're not *supposed* to eat it. It's a potion I'm making out of a powerful lichen which stimulates the mind. Its effects are dramatic. I've seen people jump over cliffs after drinking the juices, because they think something terrible is after them. There's never anything there, except perhaps a mouse. It makes everything bigger and louder and brighter. I thought a few drops might do something for Rowanne.'

'Shock her out of it, you mean?'

'Sort of.'

'Well, can you give her a nice mentality while you're at it?' enquired Fleabag. 'Turn her into a cat-lover so she can treat me with the respect I deserve.'

'She already *does* treat you as you deserve,' observed Gemma. 'Can you eat that fish in the other room with the horses or, even better, outside altogether? I can't stand the sound of you chewing when I'm so hungry!'

With a 'humph' of disgust, Fleabag picked up his particularly juicy fishhead and stalked out, tail erect and fur fluffed. The reception he got from the horses was fairly similar and he ended up behind the woodpile in disgrace.

'What happens if she goes and does something daft and we can't stop her? She's very strong.' Gemma was worried.

'I don't really know. I reckon in her state it will need quite a lot to waken her at all. She's been like this for almost three weeks now. She's hardly moved and her muscles will be weak. She hasn't eaten much either, so I reckon we could hold her down.'

Gemma wasn't happy. 'How long does it take for the effects to wear off?'

'Usually about a day, but you can get flashbacks for up to a year.'

'Is it worth the risk?' Gemma asked quietly. 'Is there something a bit milder in your bag? Something a bit less drastic?'

Phelan spread out the pile of toadstools. 'It's very difficult to find anything once the snow falls, but there's a small wood in a hollow over the ridge. It's sheltered from the mountain wind and feels a lot milder.' He picked up a white puffball that looked soft and delicate. 'This one is called "Dreamcloud". It's a sleep inducer. And this,' he held up a thick liver-like fungus about the size of his hand, 'is delicious if fried, especially with fish, but it won't help Rowanne today. These orange ones I can dry and we can eat them at a pinch. They aren't poisonous, but they're very chewy and taste like old socks. It depends how hungry we get.'

'Oh look, that one on the floor! I know that, it's a mushroom. That's clever of you to find it at this time of year.'

'Er . . .' his thin hands grabbed towards the small brown fungus which he had tried to keep out of sight. '. . . don't touch it. It's "deathcap".' Then he said nothing else.

'What does that do?' asked Gemma doubtfully.

'There's enough poison in that to kill half of Prince Rupert's army and make the other half very sick.'

'Ugh!' she jumped back. 'What did you pick that for?'

Phelan hung his head. 'In case . . . in case of a lot of things.'

He went back to stirring the pot vigorously. At last the lichen was reduced to a smooth, greyish sludge in the bottom of the pot. He put two drops of the stuff into a cup of water and stirred it. 'Feed her this on a spoon. If she starts coming to, then stop straight away. I don't want her going crazy.'

Gemma took the cup and picked up the spoon. Suddenly she had such a stabbing pain in her hands that she dropped everything.

'Hey, watch out!' moaned Phelan. 'I had to climb a difficult tree to get that bark, then it took me hours to get that mixture just right. Don't go flinging it around!'

'What's the matter?' inquired Fleabag, sliding his sleek fur around the doorpost. 'Pooh! what's that stink?'

'That "stink",' Phelan said, huffily, 'was the potion I've just spent hours brewing to try to revive Rowanne. Now Gemma's just flung half of it away.'

Gemma hung her head. 'I'm sorry. It's just that something seemed to stab right into my hands.'

'Let's have a look,' said Fleabag, climbing into Gemma's lap. She opened her palms, but there was nothing there—no mark or swelling. Fleabag sniffed her hands and licked them a little.

'Never mind,' said Phelan. 'I have more. Just be

careful this time, will you? Pass the cup.'

Fleabag put a paw on Gemma's arm. 'Wait. When Phelan passes you the mixture, just hold the cup for a minute and see what happens.'

Gemma looked at the cat. 'You're odd,' she said.

'Not as odd as I suspect *you* are,' he retorted. 'Just do as you're told, will you?'

Phelan mixed the potion again and passed Gemma the cup. Nothing happened.

'Now, bring the cup slowly towards Rowanne...'

'Ouch!' Gemma jerked her arms back, again spilling everything. 'I felt as if I was being burned!'

Fleabag sniffed at her hands again. 'I know what it is,' he announced triumphantly. 'It's the Ring Fire. That's what it is. The little bit of Fire the Fire Wielder gave you is warning you not to give that stuff to Rowanne. It's wrong for her.'

Gemma and Phelan looked wide eyed at the cat. Then Phelan looked wide-eyed at Gemma.

'You mean you have the Ring Fire, and I've been treating you just like—just like *anyone!* I... I've even been rude to you... I'm sorry, I'm so sorry!' And before Gemma knew it, he was on his knees.

'Oh, don't be stupid!' Gemma was frightened. 'I *am* "just anyone". If a street child can't be friends with a thief, what good is anything? I'd have no friends then, except this disgusting cat who keeps trying to make me eat rat...'

'It was a very *fresh* rat,' muttered Fleabag.

'... and what good are friends on their knees? I need people who are rude to me. Get up and insult me again, for goodness' sake! Can't you see I'm frightened?'

165

Fleabag curled up under Gemma's chin and purred. 'What are you getting upset about? You often get a burning in your palms when something is wrong, don't you? So why shouldn't it be the Ring Fire warning you not to give the potion to Rowanne?'

'Because the Ring Fire is back at the palace with the Fire Wielder.'

'Except for the little bit that I saw him give you. The bit he told you never to forget.'

Gemma opened her cupped hands and looked at them. They looked like ordinary hands, stained and calloused from hard work. Indeed, they *were* very ordinary hands—except that in her palms there burned a tiny speck of flame!

22

Ring Fire!

As everyone stared at the tiny flame in Gemma's cupped hands, it seemed to fade slightly as her hands began to tremble.

'Hold it! Hold it steady!' commanded Fleabag. 'Think of the Fire Wielder... Think of the Queen... Hold it!'

Gemma's hands steadied, but tears began to stream down her cheeks. 'I'm scared,' she whispered. 'Help me!'

'The Ring Fire only stays where it is welcome,' said Fleabag quietly. 'Do you want to hold it?'

'Yes.' Gemma's voice came choked and hoarse. 'It is so beautiful and calm. I want it, but I'm scared of it as well.'

Phelan and Fleabag held their breath, staring with wide eyes as the little flame in Gemma's hands grew stronger and steadier. Even Rowanne had her eyes open. She seemed to be aware of the tiny light. Gemma brought it closer for her to see.

Rowanne opened her mouth as if she was trying to say something, but couldn't.

'There,' said Gemma. 'Would you like to hold it?'

She opened the knight's hand and tried to place the flame in it. The little light would not stay; it slid like a bright jewel back into Gemma's palm. But where the flame had touched her, Rowanne's hand began to move.

'Look at that!' gasped Phelan. 'Do it again, Gemma...'

This time Gemma placed the flame into Rowanne's other hand. The same thing happened. Rowanne's eyes opened wide with longing.

Fleabag said very softly, 'It was her mind he tried to take. Try putting the flame onto her head...'

The room was heavy with silence. Trembling with anxiety, Gemma lifted the flickering little light to Rowanne's face and moved it gently across the knight's forehead to rest in front of her eyes. 'Wake up, Rowanne, wake up,' she said softly.

'As I said,' murmured Phelan, as Rowanne stirred and sat up, 'it needed something greater than magic.'

23

King of the Castle

Over the next few days Rowanne quickly regained her strength. From the moment they had left the burning Hall, she had been aware of what was happening all around her, but she had had no ability to move or respond. She had spent almost three weeks trapped inside the cocoon of her own body—a terrible situation for one so accustomed to command.

She had lost a great deal of weight, having only taken soup and water for all that time. Fleabag celebrated the return of his arch-enemy by leading a small mountain goat and her kid to their cottage, so Rowanne had milk to drink as well as the usual rabbit and fish.

It was not long before she was up and about, and taking her share in the daily tasks.

One day, Rowanne and Gemma came toiling up the steep slope to the cottage with huge bundles of firewood piled on top of the branches of what looked like half a tree they were dragging home. They were rosy cheeked and laughing as they struggled along, singing an old song in the afternoon sun. Heavy snow clouds were gathering in the sky around the mountain tops; the tracks they were making would soon be covered by snow.

As they came nearer, Phelan could see that Fleabag was riding on top of the wood, clinging on for dear life. 'I'm the King of the Castle!' he proclaimed.

'Get down, you dirty rascal!' laughed the others. Gemma tried to shove him off and Rowanne wiggled the boughs until Fleabag lost his balance and fell upside down in the snow.

'Is that the way to treat your future King?' asked the cat. 'Little do you know I've been hiding the Queen's Ring under a knot in my fur for months. Tomorrow I will produce it and astound you all. Then I'll have your heads cut off for insubordination, then you can all come to my coronation feast.'

'We won't be able to eat much if we've had our heads cut off!' complained Rowanne.

'That's the idea, of course. All the more for me.' At this the laughing cat gave an enormous jump in the air. But the somersault did not work and turned into a flop into the snow.

Having completely lost his dignity, Fleabag began to chase his tail, spinning round and round and making the soft snow fly into a small blizzard.

'You know,' Phelan said thoughtfully, 'I think Fleabag ought to be King. He'd make people laugh and forget their worries. Everyone would be happier. Too many people went in fear of Prince Rupert and his henchmen, and I'm glad the Ring wasn't found in his palace. He rules by fear and force—that's not what being a king is about.'

As soon as he stopped speaking he realized he had

insulted the cousin and fiancé of the Lady Knight. Half of him wished he could have swallowed his words. The other half was glad it had been said.

Rowanne went very pale and still. For a few seconds he was quite afraid that she would lash out at him.

Then she breathed deeply. 'You're quite right. While I couldn't speak or move, I did a lot of thinking. I'm so ashamed that I was a part of all that once. I'm sorry, Phelan—for everything: for the things I have said to you, and about your parents. When we get back, I'd like you to work for me. I have a great deal to do in Rupertsberg. You know what's most needed there. Will you help?'

He felt a lump come into his throat and pretended to be too busy to talk as he tugged the wood inside. 'Hurry up,' he called, 'Let's get this wood in the dry before the snow starts again.'

That evening Gemma made a venison stew. The onions and turnips they had bought from the nearest croft were rather bruised and soft, but the taste was heavenly after a hard day's work collecting wood. Everyone agreed the gravy needed a good hunk of homemade bread, but that was not to be had, so they all drank the juices from their bowls and felt content.

'What will happen when the Ring is found?' asked Gemma. 'Will the finder automatically become the King or Queen at once?'

Rowanne shifted her position and looked thoughtful. 'I don't think so. The Fire Wielder told us it had been hidden where only a King or Queen would dare to look, so it is unlikely that anyone else would find it. But the Ring will have to be taken back to the Hall of Light to be formally identified by those that know it.' (Here Gemma's face burned, but she said nothing.) 'Then the Fire will have to be put back in the Ring. It won't go into a Ring that isn't the right one, and if the wrong person is holding it, the Fire will fade. The Ring doesn't *make* a monarch—it just confirms the right person for everyone to see.'

'What *is* the Ring Fire?' asked Gemma nervously.

To everyone's surprise, Phelan started to speak. 'It comes from somewhere else—not another planet, just another place. It is more than goodness and truth and all that sort of thing: it is alive as well. I heard tell once that it is the heart of the Fire Giver, watching over us. Who knows?'

Rowanne looked at him curiously. 'Where did a thief-lad learn that?'

Phelan hung his head and mumbled. 'Nowhere. I just heard.'

And he would say no more.

Fleabag did not like the uneasy silence that followed. 'When I am King,' he said loudly, 'I shall have Gemma come and cook for me every day. Since we have had her in charge of the cooking pot I have almost gone off mouse.'

'Only almost,' chuckled Gemma, 'I saw you this morning with a nice fat one you were having for breakfast.'

'That wasn't mouse. That was shrew!' roared Fleabag indignantly. 'I'll make a rule about everyone having extra lessons in telling a mouse from a shrew. Vitally important, that will be. Yes, I must make a note of that,' he muttered, as he licked some gravy from behind his whiskers. Then he settled into a more comfy spot, wrapped his tail around his head and went to sleep.

Rowanne was watching Phelan out of the corner of her eye. She could see he was upset and she desperately wanted to make him feel better: 'I meant what I said earlier, you know,' she said. 'I really would like your help to put things right.'

Phelan felt confused by her offer. 'I'll think about it,' was all he would say.

'Will you marry the Prince?' asked Gemma, changing the subject.

'Goodness me, no!' laughed the lady knight. 'I think I knew I wouldn't as soon as he asked me. Although,' she hung her head, 'I was taken with the idea for a while...'

'But if you don't marry him, how will you bring about all these changes you are planning?'

'Ah!' said Rowanne with great satisfaction. 'That's the really good part. As a close member of the family, I have the right to challenge him to his title.'

'What sort of challenge?'

'It's usually sword fighting or wrestling, but it could be chess. Any contest of skill, really. Three challenges are held and the winner of two out of the three may take the title.'

'And what if you don't win?' asked Gemma, quite pale.

Rowanne looked serious. 'If I can't beat an idiot like him, then I don't deserve to rule the city. But if I do win, it can go back to its old name of Erbwenneth. I'll have none of this Rupertsberg nonsense when I'm Princess. And another thing, I can't believe that

Queen Sophia knew what was happening there, for I'm sure she wouldn't have stood for it. So I'll insist that the monarch comes to visit at least once a year.'

'It'll be a pleasure,' came Fleabag's fur-muffled voice from next to the fire.

24

Phelan Turns Back

Now that Rowanne was well enough to look after Gemma and to help with hunting and repairs, Phelan became more and more quiet and withdrawn. The snow was becoming thicker and each fall lasted longer. Wolves could be heard howling in the mountains behind the cottage.

'Doesn't "Phelan" mean "wolf"?' asked Rowanne one night.

Despite the warm crackling fire, Phelan shivered. 'Yes, but it's not a name I'd have chosen. Wolves are yet another thing that I'm frightened of. I think I had a different name when I was a child, but I can't remember it.

' "Phelan" was what the thieves called me when they took me in—I was grey all over with dirt and had long matted hair. I'd been living rough for quite a while.'

'Would you like to be called something else?' Gemma asked kindly.

'Like Catslayer!' chipped in Rowanne mischievously.

'No. Phelan will do fine—unless I discover who I

really am one day... I don't think I'd answer to anything else.'

'What do you mean about discovering who you really are?' Gemma asked.

Phelan shrugged. 'I know my parents ran a shop that sold bits and pieces—old furniture and junk, I remember that. I don't mean I'm anyone special. Far from it. It's just that when they were killed, I was forced to become someone I'm not. I didn't *like* being a thief; it was just the only way I could survive. At first it was fun—being big and brave and macho like the others. But I think we all ended up unhappy.

'One of the men had been a goldsmith. He'd been muddled up in a fraud and although he realized what he had done was wrong, he didn't dare go back. All that skill wasted. He was utterly miserable and frustrated.

'Another was a farmer—and a good one by all accounts. He was chased off his land by Rupert's soldiers. The Prince wanted the land to build a pleasure garden, of all things! The farmer had nowhere else to go but the woods. It turned him strange. He had been a decent bloke once but he became the most vicious and mean of the lot. He was convinced that everyone was out to get him, and that we were all after the bits and pieces he had put together over the years. It was frightening to watch.'

'But what about *you*, Phelan?' urged Gemma. 'Who would *you* like to be?'

He shrugged. 'I don't really know. Most of all in the world I want to get a job and find friends. I want to be able to live without hurting people.' He thought for a moment, 'I could do something like Aelforth at the hostel, maybe. Then I'd feel as if I was being useful for once, instead of destroying all the time.'

Rowanne was about to make her offer again, but she felt that now was not the time. If he wanted to be her steward in Rupertsberg, he would when he was ready.

Fleabag jumped into Phelan's lap. 'I'll employ you as tummy scratcher if you like. You will be paid in dead rats and a few fleas when I can spare them!'

Phelan laughed and pushed the incorrigible cat back onto the floor.

Long after the others were asleep, Phelan lay awake thinking. What was worrying him most was that he felt uncomfortable. Suddenly he was in the company of a Knight of the Queen's Guard who wanted him to work for her, a highly intelligent talking cat and worst of all, someone who carried the Ring Fire. He did not *belong* with them. They were special and important. He felt small and out of place.

By dawn he realized he wanted to leave. Now Rowanne was strong again they did not need him. He knew he could no longer follow them at a distance. The icy winter closing in all around meant that he would not survive in the mountains on his own.

He would have to go away and never see them again.

Phelan sighed and stood up. He went to the outside door and looked out into the night. By starlight he could see where the hills became mountains. It all looked very lonely and forbidding.

He would have to go at dawn. If he left before they got up, he could walk to one of the villages on the plain by nightfall. There must be a farmer or a workman somewhere who needed another hand. He would work for his food and shelter and wouldn't ask for money.

When spring came he could think again. He crept back into the room where the animals were stabled. He milked the goat and drank the warm sweet liquid. He tried to think. There was nothing he needed to take with him. After all, he had nothing anyway. He knew Rowanne would not begrudge him the cloak she had given him. That was all.

Then he remembered the deathcap toadstool he had left to dry in a gap in the wall. He slipped that into his pocket. He would rather eat that than be caught by wolves; its effect was very swift.

He went back to the fire and sat in a corner. There he dozed a little until the first pale streaks of light coming under the door roused him.

Softly, Phelan stepped over the sleeping Gemma and Rowanne, but he had not counted on Fleabag having a pre-breakfast nibble so early. The cat was just washing his paws and talking to Porridge, the more intelligent of the two ponies, when Phelan stumbled over him.

'Where are you off to?' challenged the cat.

'I . . . I decided to try to go down to one of the farms to buy hay for the horses. There's no grass worth speaking of now. And while I was out, I was going to try to buy a bag of flour. Gemma was saying how she missed bread.'

Fleabag picked at a flea for dessert and said,

'You'd better take the horse and the pack pony for that lot. How much money did Rowanne give you?'

'Bother that cat,' thought Phelan. 'Why does he never mind his own business?'

'Er, oh, I forgot the money.'

Fleabag immediately went to call Rowanne.

Phelan considered just bolting out of the door, but he would not get far, even with a horse. He stayed where he was.

The inner door creaked open. Rowanne was standing in front of him, stiff and bleary-eyed. 'How much do you need?'

From the depths of the cottage Gemma called out, 'A sack of flour and two bales of hay will come to about 19 groats. If you can buy some vegetables as well, it would be good. We're getting low and I've bought everything the crofters have for sale. Give him three silver pieces, Rowanne.'

The knight counted out the money. Phelan did not want to take it. But he had been caught out by his own lie. He calmed himself. Once he was out of sight, he could stop and think.

'None of the farmers between here and the marshes has anything to spare. They scarcely have enough to keep themselves alive. I will go further afield today—I may even ride to one of the villages—so if I am not back at nightfall, don't worry.'

And with that, he led the horse and the pack pony outside.

It was a glorious morning. The sun was shining in an intensely blue sky. Everything was clean and brilliantly white after another fall of fresh snow.

The horses danced a little, glad to be out of the cramped stable.

Hiding the turmoil of his feelings, Phelan turned and waved cheerfully at the others.

The horses picked their way gingerly down to the road below. With one more wave, Phelan turned southward.

Gemma went back inside and sat by the fire. She began to poke at it miserably.

'What's the matter?' purred Fleabag rubbing his fur against her leg.

'I shouldn't have let him go.'

'Why's that?' asked the cat, jumping into her lap and curling up.

'He's miserable. I'm sure he thinks we don't need him and can't possibly want him. I'm scared he won't come back.'

'Are your hands burning?'

'Not yet.'

'Well,' Fleabag stretched out to get the most heat on his tummy fur, 'I suggest you stay just where you are for a bit, so I can have my between-breakfasts doze. Then, if and when your hands start warning you something is wrong, we'll go and see what's what!'

Gemma lifted the cat from her lap and put him onto her blanket. 'Oh, you're useless,' she moaned, and went outside to stare blankly at the tracks in the snow.

25

Trapped!

Phelan rode for about two miles. The snow was not deep except where it had drifted in great frozen waves against hedges and walls. Everywhere was dazzling white in the brilliant sunshine. Far ahead, he could see where the rough land gave way to marshes and then to tamer country. A few poor crofts lay scattered across the wild terrain. They had bought supplies there before, but the land was poor and people were heavily taxed on their produce. Even gold could not buy what wasn't there.

As he made his way further and further from the cottage, he began to worry. The others would be depending on these supplies. Could he get them, leave them outside the door and slip away again? No. Daylight was too short. It couldn't be done in the time. And tomorrow he might not have the courage.

Anyway, now Rowanne was strong again, she could go and buy what was needed.

He reined the mare to a halt and looked around. Soon the land would become easier. He could ride fast—faster if he left the pack pony here. If he took her with him she would slow his progress but, on the other hand, he could sell her. She must be worth something.

Just then he heard the sound of hoofbeats behind him. Cantering down the steep road towards him were Rowanne and Fleabag on Porridge. The pony was thoroughly enjoying the run. Her sturdy legs were sending a cloud of powdery snow high into the crisp sunlit air.

Rowanne waved enthusiastically. 'Wait for us!' she called. Then she caught sight of his miserable face and hesitated. 'I hope you didn't mind us coming. It is such a glorious morning for a ride and we gave you so many errands it didn't seem fair to make you do it all.'

'What she means,' chimed in Fleabag, 'is that she didn't want to miss all the fun of a day out.'

Phelan shrugged. He began to think quickly. He could lose her easily enough. But perhaps he ought to play along just for today. They did need a lot of things and goodness only knew what the next two months would be like. The others would need plenty of supplies. How could he live with himself knowing he had left a carrier of the Ring Fire snowed in with little or no food?

He smiled sheepishly at Rowanne. 'Sorry. Just lost in my thoughts. Will Gemma be all right on her own?'

Rowanne turned round in the saddle and shielded her eyes against the glare of the snow. 'She's just coming. She shouldn't be long, it's not far and it's all downhill.'

Within a few minutes, another large black dot high up the road showed that Gemma was on the way. Fleabag jumped onto Pudding's back and whispered a few words of horse speech into her ear. Without hesitating the pony began to clamber back up the slope to meet Gemma.

'Why can that cat make Pudding do as she's told when I can't?' Phelan wondered out loud.

'I suspect he makes terrible threats involving finding new homes for his fleas under Pudding's saddle-cloth or something,' Rowanne replied. 'Anyway, here they come.'

The four of them rode downhill for about an hour. The road was slippery where snow had thawed and refrozen in patches. The sun was getting high and they stopped to eat. While the others were chewing dried meat and laughing at Fleabag's plans for when he would be King, Phelan sat unhappily on a rock and surveyed the landscape. Any other day, he would have said how beautiful everything looked. Today he just measured the distance between himself and the nearest village.

They had passed two or three small crofts on the way down, but the next stretch of road was rocky and uncultivated. Crossing that would take another hour or more. Then there was the marshy area with a few buildings fairly close to the road on a little rise. Everything looked very tumble-down and poor. The crofters probably had nothing to sell.

Phelan vaguely noted it would be a good place to aim for when he did run away. There might not be food or work, but at least he could get shelter. He would have to take his chance when he could.

He was prodded from his reverie by Rowanne's boot. 'Time to be on the road again. We don't want to risk being out after dark.'

He shivered at the thought. Taking a deep breath, hoping it would give him courage, he jumped down from his rocky perch to where the horses were waiting. But the snow had an underlayer of ice. As he landed, Phelan slipped and fell, catching his foot in a crack in the rock.

For what seemed like a long time he lay there, feeling the pain throbbing through his body.

After a while he opened his eyes. Rowanne eased him into a sitting position. 'Are you all right?'

Gemma knelt by his foot and gently tried to ease it from the cleft. It was tightly jammed. She reached down and loosened the thongs which tied his shoe. If he could get his foot out, it did not matter if he lost the shoe. But that did not work either. For what seemed ages, they tugged and wriggled at his foot until he cried out in pain.

Rowanne rummaged in her pack until she found her dagger—the same one that Phelan's gang had missed—and tried to gouge some of the looser chunks of rock free. But she only succeeded in snapping the blade.

'Bother!' she hissed. 'Look, I'll go onto the next farm and see if I can borrow a hammer or a crow-bar—or preferably both. There's only a few more hours of daylight left, and we don't want to get caught here. I've seen a lot of tracks in the snow; I fear the wolves are running low.'

'Well, tell them from me that the cat is running high!' replied Fleabag fluffing out his chest fur. 'I used to be known as "Wolfbane" in my youth!'

Gemma grinned at Fleabag's bravado. 'I'll stay with Phelan,' she volunteered.

'So will I,' added Fleabag. 'He might need some-one to protect him.'

'I can't think of anyone I'd less rather have if I were in a spot,' Rowanne jibed. 'You're all quips—and no equipment!'

Fleabag pretended that he hadn't heard, but his tail twitched irritably.

'Come on, cat!' called Gemma. 'Help me find firewood. At least we can keep warm while we're waiting.

Alone at last, Phelan sat still and closed his eyes. In his imagination he saw snarling wolves with saliva dripping from pointed teeth. He opened his eyes again and concentrated on looking up at the sky. The sun was well past its zenith and heavy clouds were beginning to blow across the sky.

He could think of nothing but the cold, and the fear of what would happen when night fell. He mustn't endanger the others. If he were dead, then they would *have* to leave him and go home.

He felt in his pocket for the deadly toadstool. Nothing. He rummaged in the other pocket. Still nothing... Yet he remembered picking it up and putting it in there. Had he dropped it? Please, no ... if someone thought it was a shrivelled mushroom and put it in the pot for tonight's supper... No, he mustn't let himself think like that. It must have fallen out onto the snow.

The important thing was that the fungus wasn't there. He was well and truly trapped and the others would be bound to be heroic and stay with him. When night fell, the wolves would get them all.

The sunlight had gone. The day was growing

colder and darker. Phelan sat up and looked around. Dusk was several hours away. The darkness came from more snow clouds. He was getting very cold. Even his thick cloak was no real protection from the wind.

Once more he wriggled forward and examined his ankle. He had hoped that if he stayed still and did not tug at it, the swelling would go down so he could ease his foot out. He was pretty sure it was only sprained. If only he could get it free, they all still stood a chance.

Taking a handful of snow, he rubbed it as far down his leg as he could reach to reduce any swelling. But the touch of the snow burned him painfully and his foot remained as stuck as ever.

He swung his arms wildly and rubbed himself all over to keep warm. The wind was beginning to whip up and he knew that if the wolves did not get to him, the cold would.

Once more he searched his pockets, vainly hoping that amongst the dusty lint and bits of string there might be something useful. Nothing.

Phelan closed his eyes again and told his fears to go away. He must think of something good. He must not let his last hours be filled with horror and regret.

He thought of the Ring Fire dancing in Gemma's hand. It made him feel as if there might be hope.

Suddenly it occurred to him, that if the Ring were not found, the Fire would fade. That would mean the end of hope not only for him. There would be utter misery throughout the land. Without it everyone would feel as empty and desolate as he felt now. It must be the Ring Fire that made sure a good king or queen sat on the throne. Without it, there would be war and tyrants everywhere.

It was then that he made a decision. If he got out of this alive, he *would* stay with his friends and help them find the Ring. Perhaps he *could* do something—even something as mundane as helping them survive the winter or fight off other robbers. He would do what he could to help. Even if he was just a thief, for once, Phelan was going to be someone who *did* something instead of running away all the time.

He pulled his cloak around himself and wished the others were back. Brave decisions needed brave friends to help keep courage alive.

It was not long before he heard Gemma and Fleabag cheerfully poking fun at each other as they hauled sticks and brushwood back to where he sat.

That was something. Wolves were frightened of fire.

He helped to snap the wood into kindling and twigs while Gemma went back to gather more. He selected a few strong, straight branches and rubbed the stick ends against the rock until they had sharp points. At a pinch the sticks could be jabbed at an animal's eyes. He would fight as long as he was able to.

He must not let himself be afraid. Wolves could smell that in a man's sweat. If he concentrated on good things, the fear smell might not be so bad and they might not come.

For once in his life, Phelan knew he must not let himself be afraid.

26

Wolf Pack

The sound of the wolves howling in the foothills behind them mingled with the whistle of the wind as the beginnings of yet another blizzard swept down to the plains below. Daylight would soon be gone. An unhappy greyness hung in the air.

Rowanne led the mare by the head and bowed before the blast, clutching her cloak around her. The horse stumbled through the soft, ever-deepening snow. Bundled on the animal's back were faggots of wood collected on the way.

The crofter had no tools he was willing to lend or sell. He had given Rowanne short shrift. Now they were left with nothing but their wits to keep Phelan alive in the teeth of a mid-winter blizzard. Painfully cold, she struggled the last few steps to where Gemma, Fleabag and Phelan sat huddled under their cloaks.

The two ponies had been tethered under a small overhang behind them. It was not close enough to share warmth, but one good fire should keep the wolves away from them all.

To Rowanne's surprise, although there was a

good pile of wood ready to light, it had been left cold and wet, with the snow-spotted figures shivering miserably next to it.

'Thank goodness you're here,' mewed Fleabag pitifully. 'Phelan forgot to bring a tinder-box and Gemma has worn her hands raw trying to get the wood to light with a spindle.'

'I'll be with you in a minute,' called Rowanne, as she threw the new wood down and led the horse away to shelter with the others. When she came back, Gemma pulled a few bits of kindling out from under her cloak where she had been keeping them dry.

Just then snuffling and heavy breathing made the horses rear and whinny in terror.

'Light something, Rowanne,' hissed Fleabag from his depths. 'Light it quickly!'

The first sparks from her tinder box failed, but soon a small flicker of orangey-yellow light caught in the tiny twigs. The first glimmers of fire caught the bright gold reflections from the eyes of a young wolf.

Rowanne pulled out her handkerchief and let it catch light. Then she wound it around a stick and jabbed it in the direction of the animal until, with a flurry of snow, it turned tail and ran into the blizzard.

With the last remains of the fire she began to coax a few larger twigs alight until there was a small, but comforting blaze. 'Keep it going,' she instructed Phelan. 'I'm going to get some things from the saddle-bags.'

Gemma went to help unsaddle the animals and pulled blankets over the horses' backs. Rowanne carried the saddles back to the fire. It was warmer sitting on the well worn leather than the ice-cold stone. She had no real supplies with her. After all, they had not expected to be out after dark.

From the position he was in, Phelan could not sit on a saddle, but Rowanne managed to feed a log underneath him.

'My ears are cold,' moaned the cat.

'You'll be nice and snug in a wolf's tummy in a minute,' muttered Rowanne. 'Try sorting out small twigs. That'll keep you warm.'

Gemma pulled a nicely burning stick from the fire and peered all around for signs of wolves, holding the torch high and letting its yellow light toss in the wind. But a strong gust, heavy with wet snow, quickly put the flame out.

Only a few strides away, a wolf-shadow stopped and stared at the smoking stick. It hesitated and stepped backwards. As it turned to run, Rowanne lunged after it and caught it in the belly with her sword. Swiftly she dispatched it and flung the carcass further down the hill. Now the smell of blood would bring the rest of the pack. She did not know whether they would feed on the flesh of one of their own and be satisfied, or if they would seek human, horse- or even cat-flesh . . .

She did not have long to consider the matter, for out of the darkness came more long, low shadows with the distinctive musty smell of wolfkind.

The dusk was deepening every second. Rowanne turned to the fire, which seemed to be losing the struggle for life in the teeth of the ice, cold and wet. One by one the tiny flames winked yellow, orange, then red as they cooled and died. Phelan was leaning sideways, holding his cloak as a shelter from the wind. But it was not enough.

Gemma's benumbed fingers struggled again and again with the tinder box as she tried to light the last few dry wood-shavings. 'It's no good!' She flung it down, almost crying. 'I can't get the kindling to catch!'

'Let me have a go,' offered Phelan. 'Hold the cloak up, will you?'

For several minutes he struggled. 'I think the flint must be wet. I can't even get a spark.'

Rowanne swore angrily. 'Gemma, take my sword. I'll do it.' But everything was getting colder and wetter by the second. Her fingers reddened and swelled until she could hardly bend them.

'Rowanne?' Gemma called nervously. 'I think the wolves are coming closer.'

'I can smell them,' Fleabag added. 'They are frightened. They always smell strongest when they are scared. We must get the fire going.'

'Easier said than done,' Rowanne hissed as she renewed her efforts with the flint and iron.

Suddenly she lost her grip completely and the little box rattled down the crevasse which held Phelan captive. 'Oh!' she gasped. 'Oh, I'm so sorry!'

No one could see down the black gouge of the crack. It was now almost completely dark. Even the intense white glow of snow had faded in the eternal grey smudge of the blizzard. Fleabag sprang forward and pushed his paw down the hole. 'It is too deep for me,' he said.

Phelan leaned forwards and pushed his fingers down. 'I think I can touch it, but I can't pick it up.

It's fallen to one side, so I can't poke it out with a stick or anything. Can you have a go, Gemma? You have the smallest hands.'

Gemma, who was trying very hard to say nothing harsh to Rowanne, slid her achingly cold fingers down the crack, but she could feel nothing except burning ice. How she wished she could feel the comforting warmth of the Ring Fire again. She sat up and wrapped her hand in the folds of her cloak. She bit her lip and rubbed her skin gently, but the pain throbbed relentlessly, and her fingers would not even bend.

Rowanne passed a small flask of spiced cordial around in silence.

'Why don't you three ride back to the cottage?' urged Phelan, trying to be brave. 'You still stand a chance if you go back now, but none at all if you stay here.'

'We couldn't do it in the dark and snow,' Rowanne replied. 'If I'd realized earlier on in the day just how difficult it was going to be, I'd have gone back for all sorts of things. But our only chance now is to stick together.'

'Are your fingers warm enough to have another go at finding the tinder-box yet?' asked Phelan.

Gemma tried, but was met by the most painful aching cold she had ever experienced. She sat back on her heels and squeezed her hands under her armpits, rocking with the burning agony and trying not to cry. Tears would freeze on her face and make things even worse.

Rowanne was glad no one could see the worried look on her face. She was a trained knight. She had been sent to protect Gemma. Somehow they must survive—it was her responsibility. 'Has anyone got any weapons of any kind?' she asked.

'My fifteen claws are the sharpest in the kingdom,' Fleabag announced proudly. 'They have put out the eyes of many of the Queen's foes!'

'I've got some sharpened sticks,' offered Phelan. 'If we sort through the firewood for the strongest, straightest boughs, we could make some more. Has anyone got a knife?'

Rowanne handed over the broken dagger blade. 'That's about all it's fit for now,' she said, peering into the deepening gloom where the low, dark shadows of wolf pelts seemed to be ever multiplying. The beasts were crouched quite still. It was as if they knew their moment would come. All they had to do was wait.

As the scent of wolf grew stronger, one of the ponies whinnied and began to tug at her rope. Gemma got up and pulled a rug across the pony's back, talking gently to the animal all the time. It crossed her mind that if she took the rug from the pony, it might help keep Rowanne and Phelan warmer. But she couldn't bring herself to do it. Poor Porridge was shivering with cold and terror as it was. And should they find a way to free Phelan's foot, they would need all the ponies to be warm and alive to escape from the wolves.

Gemma smoothed her face against the animal's neck. It made her feel better and warmer. For a while she stayed that way. Perhaps they could all take turns to warm up like this during the night. It might keep them going—except for poor old Phelan.

Reluctantly she left the shelter of the horses to return to the slowly growing snow drift that gave them some protection from the night. Just then a long, dark shadow cut the narrow distance between her and the others.

Crouching low, the animal snarled at Gemma, trying to steer her away from the horses. If they got her a little further back, there would be high rocks behind her and a sheer drop to her left.

She glanced around in panic. The heavy smell of wet wolf hair mixed with its foul breath as the beast began to close in on her.

'Rowanne!' she whispered hoarsely, too frightened to scream in case the animal pounced. 'Rowanne! Help!'

But the howling wind carried her words away.

Just then the mare whinnied and shied, lashing out with her forehooves. After a few seconds, Porridge and Pudding did the same. But they were too well tethered to do any good.

The noise was enough, though, to rouse Rowanne from her icy state of near-exhaustion. Fleabag leaped out too and bristled his fur so he looked about three times his normal size. But between Gemma and her friends was a semicircle of deadly hunters, merciless and hungry.

Gemma took a step or two to the side. The wolves swayed that way too. Then she took a step back. The black, stinking bodies began to crowd in closer.

The horses began their cacophony again. They tugged at their ropes as they tried to flee in panic. But all they could do was roll their eyes and scream horribly.

Rowanne threw back her head and yelled as she drew her sword and began to lunge at the wolves from behind.

But as she did so, Phelan flung the first of his wooden spears in the opposite direction.

They were surrounded.

Gemma froze with horror. No one could help her. None of them could help any one else. The wolves had succeeded in separating the travellers from each other.

She felt sick as she heard Pudding howling in pain as one of the wolves sank his fetid, yellow teeth into her leg, or perhaps it was her neck . . . who knew?

Anyway, it was too late.

27

The Burning

Suddenly Gemma became very, very angry. Without knowing how or why, she flung her arms open wide and yelled: 'Go away! *Go away!* How dare you attack us?' Red faced and furious, she stamped her foot very hard on the snow-covered rock.

Rowanne and Phelan watched open-mouthed. For from Gemma's hands, great plumes of orange and yellow fire streaked up into the night sky.

With howls of dismay, the whole pack of wolves turned and ran off into the night.

The snow had stopped falling and the Ring Fire had gone. Now the night was everywhere, pressing in on them with a silent blackness from which there seemed to be no escape. Gemma was still standing alone on the rocks, shaking with fear and astonishment. Fleabag ventured out from under the blanket and caught hold of her trouser leg, drawing her back toward the bivouac. 'Come into the warm. I will go and see what state Pudding is in.'

Rowanne, who had run a little way after the wolves to kill any she could reach, came panting back up the hillside. 'I'll come with you. If she is badly wounded I can kill her quickly. I won't let her suffer.'

Pudding had only a shoulder wound. Rowanne packed clean snow onto it to staunch the flow of blood. If the wolves did not attack her again she stood a good chance of surviving.

The knight cleaned the wolf-blood from her sword with snow. She dried it meticulously on her cloak and slipped it back into its scabbard.

She called Gemma to help her shift some of the wolf carcasses further away from their camp, but the girl did not answer. Rowanne called her again.

This time Phelan's voice replied: 'I think you had better come here.'

Rowanne gave up on the carcasses and climbed back to the others. Huddled under vegetable sacks and half of Phelan's cloak, Gemma was staring blankly at the pile of wood they had not been able to light.

'If—if I can make fire come—just like *that*—' she said hesitantly, '—then why shouldn't I light *this* fire?'

'Why not?' Rowanne encouraged her.

Tentatively, Gemma stretched out her hands to the pile of small twigs and thought hard about heat. But nothing happened. Then she screwed her eyes tightly closed. 'Come on, Ring Fire!' she said. 'Burn!'

She could feel the nervous, quiet breathing of the others next to her—but that was all. No crackle or snap of a burning twig.

After a while she opened her eyes and looked at the

wood, then at her hands. She could just see them in the pale luminescence of the snow. But that was all. No Ring Fire.

Angry and embarrassed, she said nothing, but snuggled between her two friends and tried to go to sleep. Numbing cold was creeping up her arms and legs and she was very tired.

Slowly the time wore on into the pitch-black, colder-than-ice dead of night. The four of them sat almost silently, taking turns from time to time to comfort the horses and warm up a little at the same time. Phelan quietly whittled at sticks to make more lethal-tipped spears, but after a while he could hold Rowanne's broken dagger no longer. He let it drop in the snow next to him.

They knew the wolves were still there in the silence of the dark, although further away than they had been. Occasionally a shadow shifted, or they heard a slight scuffle in the snow.

From time to time, Rowanne took up Gemma's spindle and socket to try to revive the fire. But apart from a slight whiff of smoke, nothing happened. They passed round the last of the food and spiced cordial, but there was still most of the night to go before dawn.

After a while, Gemma found herself dozing and dreaming about the Ring Fire in a way that was real enough to actually warm her—but she guessed it was that dangerous state of exposure when the snow begins to feel welcoming and good. She sensed that Phelan was at that stage already.

With an effort she shook her head and arms and forced herself awake.

Fleabag opened his eyes and stretched. 'What d'you do that for?' he moaned.

'What?'

'Put the fire out. We were all just beginning to get warm at last, and you put it out.'

'What are you talking about?' she asked, quite bemused. Suddenly she realized that she really *had* been warm. She put her hand out to stroke the cat's fur and that too was pleasantly hot.

Gemma shrank back into herself. This frightened her. 'What do you mean, I put the fire out?' she asked suspiciously.

'Just now,' Rowanne began, 'while you were sitting quite still, there was a warm fire glowing at your feet. It wasn't the bonfire—it just burned. No twigs or anything, just fire. But then you stirred and sat up and it was gone!' She clicked her fingers. 'Just like blowing a candle out.'

Gemma closed her eyes and shook her head. She felt so confused.

'Go on,' urged Fleabag. 'Think of the Ring Fire one more time.'

'Must I?' pleaded Gemma, terrified of failing again. But the sight of a wolf shadow shifting closer answered her own question. She looked at a space on the ground a little ahead of her. Slowly a tiny glowing light appeared. Then it grew bigger and bigger.

Slowly and gingerly, Gemma carried the precious golden flame over to the pile of wood. 'Please, burn,' she said quietly, 'or we are all wolf meat.'

Suddenly with a soft roar, the wood caught and orange flames leapt high into the night sky. With a cheering crackling and hissing noise, warmth and light began to chase the darkness backwards. Shadows retreated into themselves and the wolves howled and ran as flying sparks caught in their shaggy coats.

Rowanne and Fleabag stared in amazement and awe at Gemma's tired, pale face. She looked terrified and exhausted.

She looked at her two friends. 'Did *I* do that?' she whispered.

Neither of them answered. Then softly from behind them, Phelan said, 'The Ring Fire did it— you just allowed it to happen.'

'But why couldn't I do it the first time?'

'Because you wanted it to obey you. You were trying to force it as if you were a wizard. It's the sort of thing the Chancellor would have done. The Ring Fire obeys no one. It burns when someone allows it to do so, not when people try to *make* it happen.'

Gemma closed her eyes and remembered the Fire Wielder in the Hall of Light, giving the last bit of his strength to enable the Ring Fire to burn even though it was separated from the Royal Ring. 'Because it is welcome,' he had said.

Gemma turned to Phelan wide-eyed. He alone of all the companions did not look happy. Caught as he was by his foot, he could not run, nor even turn away. 'How *do* you know so much?' she asked gently.

There was a long silence. Phelan looked sadly into the firelight. At last he spoke, with a visible effort. 'When I said that no one would take me in after my parents died, it wasn't true. I lived with Aelforth at the Rupertsberg hostel for a while and he tried to teach me. He is a wise man. He understands things like the Ring Fire.

'But I made friends with street kids who were learning to be thieves and pick-pockets. I wanted to be big and tough like them, not quiet and gentle like Aelforth. So I ran away and lived rough until I could prove myself as a thief—then they took me in. But I really was grey and filthy. That part was no lie!'

Suddenly he smiled as he looked into the rich, warm, living gold of the flames. 'Since then I've done a lot of running away. But tonight I've promised myself that if I get out of this, I'll stay with you and help you as best I can.'

Softly the fire crackled and roared and rose up in the night sky. Phelan did not say anything else. He just leaned his head on his knees and sat quite still until dawn.

As the first light crept across the snow to the east, the flames began to die. Phelan stirred, looking around him. At last he stood up and stretched. It was then he glanced down. 'Just look at that!' he said.

The swelling on his foot had gone down. He was no longer caught in the rocks. He could stand.

Before the sun had risen the companions had re-saddled the horses and were well on their way back along the narrow road which led towards their home.

The journey back was slower because of the uphill climb. The wind had dropped and there was no more snow, but still it took them almost three hours to struggle back.

Gemma sagged on the pony's back in a state of

almost complete exhaustion. As soon as they got home, she sank into a corner by the very ordinary fire Phelan had lit with his tinder-box and slept.

Rowanne fussed over Phelan, trying to make him get some rest as well. But he did not want it. He simply sat on the doorstep, wrapped in a blanket and stared out across the empty snow. He said nothing. There were no words left to say.

Fleabag went on a little hunting trip, more because he couldn't stand the silence than out of need. He sensed that now was not the time to crack jokes. Rowanne tended to the horses, then she slept as well.

It was late in the afternoon when Phelan roused them all with a bowl of hot broth. When Rowanne asked him how he was, he just shook his head, 'It's funny, but I feel as if for the first time I'm really myself.' He looked up and smiled warmly. 'I can't tell you how good it feels.'

Gemma smiled a little from where she was still half asleep in a corner. She was glad he was happy, but everything that had happened the night before had terrified her. She ate the broth and slept again.

Two days later there was a lull in the biting northerly wind and Rowanne and Phelan went together down to the plain to get the hay, flour and vegetables they would need to see them through the long weeks ahead. Phelan said almost nothing the whole way. As they approached the place where the burning had happened, he reined in the horse and stared at the spot for a long time. 'Gemma doesn't want to believe she's carrying the Ring Fire, does she?' he asked.

Rowanne, who was riding the mare, stared at the spot and felt uncomfortable. She said nothing. Gently she urged her mount to follow in the horse's tracks and gave Pudding a tug on the leading rein.

She was not sure whether she hated or loved what was happening. One thing was clear, Gemma was more than just some street brat who would be able to identify the real Ring when she saw it.

She knew that she, the Lady Knight Rowanne de Montiland, was jealous of a street child. She wanted to be someone special too. But perhaps her importance was yet to come to light . . . Perhaps she would find the Ring—or at least be present when it was found. She must have been sent on this quest for a reason.

Anyway, her training told her there was no room for jealousy. They would have to be cooped up in two tiny rooms for another six weeks or more, and they would have to work together in order to survive. So she pushed her feelings aside and concentrated on keeping to the path in the treacherous snow.

28

The Warming

Phelan took to sitting in the morning sunshine leaning his back against the rough stone wall of the cottage. His golden-brown skin had become even more tanned with snow burn and his black curly hair and beard were getting rather long. But he carried an air of contentment that reminded Gemma of the way the old Queen had looked the day the Fire Wielder came.

One day, after sitting like this in silence for a while, Phelan leaned back and closed his eyes. Then, taking a deep breath, he began to sing. Gemma had never heard him sing before, but in rich tones, he sang an old folksong about the hope each season brought; how, at the centre of all the turning year, the Ring Fire always burned.

Gemma had been fetching water from the stream. She stopped, put the bucket down and stood transfixed, for she had never heard such a song before. It was so beautiful it brought a lump to her throat.

Even Fleabag managed to be silent for a while and listen.

When the song was finished, Phelan did not move, but opened his eyes and smiled.

Gemma found she was staring very rudely with her mouth wide open. Coming to herself suddenly, she wiped her eyes and picked up her bucket. The song had made her feel as if she was hearing the Ring Fire speak—something she had half imagined in the days when she was still the Queen's maid.

But despite the beauty of the song, Gemma did not like it. Every little reminder that she was carrying the Ring Fire in her hands worried her. She felt so small in the face of something so great that, like Phelan once, she wanted to run away from it.

She busied herself with any and every little task she could find, and even did several things twice but, however she tried to shut her feelings out, the words of Phelan's song went round and round in her head.

She was very unhappy.

The next day, Fleabag managed to get Gemma away from the others on the pretext of asking her to pick off his fleas—a task he always preferred to have done in private. It was a chilly, grey day, but the cat had carefully chosen a spot in the lee of the woodpile where they could sit in relative comfort.

Gemma patted her lap and Fleabag jumped up. But instead of immediately rolling on his back and purring as she combed through his tummy fur, he sat bolt upright and stared hard right into Gemma's eyes.

'OK,' he said sternly. 'Spill the beans. What's the matter?'

'Nothing,' said Gemma, tugging at his fur. 'You'll have to shift, I can't comb you if you don't co-operate.'

'And I can't help *you* if you don't co-operate!'

'You can't help me,' she said flatly.

'Who says?' asked the cat, head on one side and blinking his golden eyes at his friend.

Gemma began to tug the comb through the cat's neck fur. 'You don't seem to have many fleas,' she said.

''Course I haven't. I ate them all for breakfast. I just needed an excuse to get you alone.'

'So what are you going to do now? Eat me too?' Gemma was cross. She did not like being cornered. Suddenly she stood up and tried to push the cat off. but he clung on with all fifteen claws.

'Sit down!' he commanded. 'And listen! You are unhappy. A blind, half-witted field mouse could see that if he looked out of his hole backwards. And it's all because of the Ring Fire. Right? Now spill. Tell me what you are feeling, because none of this is going to go away.'

Gemma shrugged. 'It's just that ... Well ... you of all people should understand ... After all you're like me, a nobody. We're both strays. We came from nowhere and after this is done, we're *going* no-where ... Or so I thought. Suddenly I seem to have been given the most important thing in the whole world to carry ... I could cope with being timid little Gemma Streetchild who had to go on an errand for her Queen. But suddenly, I feel as if *I* have to do something as well. I don't like it. It's not me—it's too much.'

Fleabag ignored a small shrew that scuttled past Gemma's feet. 'How do you know it's not you?' he demanded. 'Who *says* you're only Gemma Streetchild? Who says I'm only a mangy old street cat? No one in the whole wide world is made to be "only" anything. Perhaps one day the Ring Fire will be given to everyone to carry—then we wouldn't need queens and laws. Wouldn't that be nice?'

Gemma laughed at this. She hadn't noticed that Phelan had come quietly round the woodpile and was watching them.

Silently he knelt in the snow next to them. Then he said, 'Bring the Ring Fire to light, Gemma. Do it now. It will cheer us all. Let it burn in your hand a little and you will feel better.'

Heart thumping, Gemma opened her hands and watched as the tiny flame flickered in the cup of her fingers. Everyone was silent for a long moment.

'It's funny,' she said softly, her head on one side, 'I had always thought of it as burning for right or wrong, or for getting rid of horrid things—but I never realized before how warming it is just to look at it. It's almost as if, in a strange way, it loves me.'

The weeks wore on slowly. The closeness of the confinement, especially on days when the weather was very bad, meant that tempers became frayed. Rowanne became increasingly officious and Fleabag took great delight in winding her up more and more every day.

Phelan and Gemma began to talk for long hours. He told her all he knew about the Ring Fire and she told him about the Queen and how kind and good she was and how it would have grieved her deeply if she had seen the oppression and injustice of Rupertsberg, or the neglect and poverty around Porthwain.

'She knew she was just too old to rule in the end. But she just didn't know how to find a successor.' Then a new thought struck her. 'Do you know how *she* was chosen? It must have been a long time ago.'

'It was well over a hundred years ago. She must have been very young then, and very old when she died. I don't know what she did to be chosen, but I believe it always has to be an action that only a king or queen would dare to do.'

Gemma nodded. 'In the same way that the Ring will be found where only a king or queen would dare to look? I remember at the Festival that the Queen said everyone was so busy trying to do noble feats they were forever missing the point of what it was all about . . .'

She hesitated. 'Phelan, what will they do if no one is found? What if the Ring is lost for ever?'

'I know Rowanne fears a lot of problems if a successor is not found within a year and a day. There will be unrest everywhere. The Prime Minister is very old, too, and with no Fire Wielder or monarch either, we could be into a very dangerous situation. I doubt if the old ways will be followed—there's really no one left to ensure that a monarch is chosen properly. I'm afraid it's more likely to end up as an unsightly scrap between the various noble families of the six provinces.'

'But what will happen to the Fire?'

'Without the Ring it will fade back to where it came from, and who knows what will happen then? But in the end it's got to be all right.' Phelan paused. 'The Fire Giver would never desert us, even if there's a long struggle ahead.'

Gemma sighed. Suddenly she remembered the Fire Wielder. How was he? Would he live to proclaim the new king or queen? He had longed to hand the Ring Fire to his own successor and, like the Queen, go to the Quiet Place in peace.

Soon everything would be settled one way or another. But what would happen to her and to Phelan? She knew she could not face going back to the kitchens, and he had no skill or trade except thieving. He would never work for Rowanne, however much she pleaded.

Fleabag would be all right. He always was. There must be many a cook who would employ his excellent ratting skills.

If Rowanne did not win the Princedom of Rupertsberg, she could go back to being a knight at court. The life suited her. It was obvious that long months cooped up in a tiny cottage with a talking cat, a thief and a guttersnipe had been a miserable experience for her.

Gemma gave up thinking about the future. It was too depressing.

But after the long tedium of endless snow, one morning came when the companions were wakened by a steady dripping. Fleabag was the first outside and minutes later he returned with wet paws and a large fish.

'It's a thaw!' he declared gleefully. 'The trout are swimming and there are birds in the sky. Spring is on its way!'

The easing of the temperature did not last long and soon fresh snow had fallen. But the thaws became more frequent and lasted longer. Phelan scraped a patch of snow away for the horses to nibble at early grass, and everyone began to feel better.

Eventually the day came when, apart from the higher hills, all the snow had gone.

The companions sat on the sun-warmed grass and watched early bees searching for nectar. High in the air an eagle soared, and the earth smelled rich and loamy.

'Time to be on the move!' announced Rowanne in her best 'campaigning' voice. 'If we leave straight away and don't stop anywhere, we'll be back in Harflorum by May with a little time in hand before the year and a day is up.'

Gemma stared at Rowanne in disbelief. The woman was standing in her riding clothes, arms folded across her leather jerkin and dark hair bound up in the woollen snood she wore under her helmet. She looked every inch the knight.

But she was looking the wrong way: back across the marshes to the plains and the way they had come.

'No,' Gemma said firmly. 'How can you even suggest going back? We go on—north by north-west.'

29

Dire Warnings

Rowanne looked at Gemma incredulously. 'But how can you even think of going on? It took six months to get from Harflorum to where we are now; there are only about nine or ten weeks left of the year and a day.

'We will get back in time if we go now—but if we go on we will have lost everything. I know you meant well, going north by north-west, but we haven't had so much as a sniff of the Ring. No sightings—not even rumours.'

Gemma stood up. She was still a lot shorter and skinnier than the knight, but she felt she could not argue sitting down. The wind flapped at her hair. She pushed it back and climbed onto a small rock so she could look Rowanne in the eye.

'I don't care if you think of me as a silly child. I did what the Ring Fire told me to do. And I will keep *on* doing it. I will go north by north-west until I can go no further. By the oath you took on your knighthood in Harflorum, you are free to leave us whenever you choose. But I will go on. Alone if necessary.' The girl's green eyes were blazing and she felt her face going red. But she had spoken and that was all that mattered.

Rowanne blinked and looked quite taken aback. Gemma had always been so timid before. 'But you can't go on,' she protested. 'You are needed at Harflorum to identify the real Ring. What happens if you don't come back in time?'

Suddenly Fleabag sprang up beside Gemma, hissing as he rubbed himself against her trouser leg.

Rowanne looked hard at the cat. 'What do *you* want?' she demanded.

The cat sat up straight and glared at his old adversary. 'You want to be in at the proclamation of the real Ring so you can be sure of getting a good position at court for yourself... Furthermore, you know that without Gemma there will be no proclamation at all, because the Fire Wielder might not be alive when we get back. You're scared of missing out for yourself! That's why you want Gemma to go back with you now!'

Rowanne lowered her head and glowered under her dark brows. She pointed a firm finger straight at the cat's head. 'I have sworn to have your pelt for a fur collar, and by all I hold precious, one day I will keep my vow!'

Fleabag just looked up at Rowanne and smirked. 'I'd like to see you try!' he said.

Just then Phelan came out of the cottage. 'What's all the noise about?' he asked.

Gemma and Rowanne both started talking at once. He could not understand a word either of them said, so he and Fleabag went down to the stream for an intelligent conversation about what was happening.

When they returned, Gemma and Rowanne had all their things spread out on the grass. They were sorting and packing furiously, but in deadly silence.

Phelan stood and watched them for a few seconds. Then, 'I'm going with Gemma,' he announced suddenly.

'So am I,' added the cat, sitting down firmly on Gemma's saddle-bag to strengthen his point.

Gemma straightened, clutching a pile of clothes in her arms. 'Rowanne, we need you. The quest for the Ring needs you. Please don't leave us.' Gemma was no longer defiant, but looked up at the woman with a child's eyes again.

The knight stopped packing and stared around at the others. Inside she was struggling. At last she sighed and bowed slightly.

'I have seen you holding the Ring Fire, Gemma. It is my duty to stay with you. If we move now, straight away, we may have enough time to go a little further.

'But there will come a day when I will spend the rest of the money Prince Rupert gave me to buy a swift horse and gallop ahead of you all back to Harflorum. It is also my sworn duty to defend the peace of this kingdom. And there will be trouble when a year and a day is up, I guarantee it. The Ring Fire will lead you as it may, but I must be at the palace for that day. Whatever else happens. On that day you will be penniless and on your own. Do you understand? I can do no more.'

'How much further can we go?' Phelan asked.

Rowanne scratched some figures on a rock with her broken dagger. 'I will accompany you for two more weeks. On the day of the vernal equinox, I must leave you.'

'Which way is north by north-west, anyway?' asked Gemma, sitting on a bag so Phelan could tie it more tightly.

'On through the mountains,' Rowanne replied, lashing a bundle of blankets onto the pack pony's pannier. 'I talked to one of the crofters the other day. He reckons the pass will be open by now and it's not a bad road anyway. We should be in the province of Beulothin within a couple of days. Apparently they have a spectacular Spring Festival and we might get to see it if we're lucky.'

'How far does north by north-west go on for?' Gemma sounded weary, despite the long months of enforced rest.

'Beulothin extends from the mountains to the sea. There's nothing else then, unless you take a ship.' Rowanne stopped tugging at cords and looked hard at Gemma. 'You're still convinced that's the way to go? How long will you keep going?'

Gemma shrugged. 'I'll keep going until I know I must stop, I suppose.'

'The Ring Fire will tell you when to stop,' said Fleabag.

Gemma smiled uncertainly. 'Maybe. I still find the Ring Fire is something too big to even think about. Sometimes the only thing I'm certain of is that I'm going on because I promised the Queen I would. I'm doing it because I loved her.'

No one felt they could say anything after that, although Phelan longed to try and be comforting. He wanted to tell her she must let the Ring Fire burn *inside* her, not just hold it at a distance in her hands . . . But now was not the time. They had to get on the road.

The road across the mountains to Beulothin was not a long one, but the travellers took it slowly because there were still many icy patches. The first evening they could still see the foothills where they had wintered.

The second night was spent in a bivouac at the top of the pass, under a canopy of blankets because it was raining. No one slept and they found nothing to eat. Miserably, they started off again very early. The road was fairly level, but wound tortuously between rockfalls and mountain streams. Before noon the path began dipping downward, then twisted and turned out of a steep-sided rift until suddenly a misty plain spread out far below them.

As the days wore on, the ground was softer and greener and the air became warmer, until they reached the plains of very rich and fertile land. Forests lay to their left and to their right were mile after mile of well-tilled fields, fat hedgerows and plenty of wildlife. They were cold and tired, but passers-by told them the city of Beriot lay straight ahead—north by north-west.

Gemma was greatly cheered by this news. She wanted to go to the city to buy good food, but she did not want to leave the right road again.

Everywhere there were signs of people preparing for the Spring Festival. Garlands were being hung from windows, bunting slung across village streets. Yet the people did not seem excited. In fact they looked terrified. They scuttled in a frightened way between houses and shops, and at the sight of the travellers they turned their backs.

Eventually they did manage to find a farmer's wife who was willing to take them in for a night. She fed them well and provided beds for all.

The thin, grey-looking woman cooked them a good breakfast and Fleabag was given cream. She seemed friendly enough, although, like everyone else, very sad. As she cleared away the plates, she asked them where they were going.

'We've come to see the Spring Festival,' replied Phelan enthusiastically. 'We've heard it's wonderful.'

The woman pulled herself up straight and looked at her visitors. 'Don't!' she said tersely. 'Don't ask why, just clear off in the other direction as fast as you can.'

The travellers looked at each other in amazement.

The woman leaned on the table and looked each of the friends in the eye. 'It's a bad business. This is no place for those who do not belong. Come to the *last* day of the festival, if you must—the day of the equinox, when there will be parties and rejoicing. But for now—take my advice if you value your lives, and *flee!*'

She stood straight again, clutching her teatowel to her thin chest.

'But what's wrong with now?' Phelan asked, disappointed.

The woman clicked her tongue and finished clearing the breakfast things noisily. Phelan paid her for their board and lodging and tried to coax more information out of her with an extra silver piece. Although she looked hungrily at the coin, she would say nothing further. She just scurried into the kitchen, from where she called out into the street that if they kept going 'steady-like' on the north by north-west road, they would surely make the festival in good time.

'Good day and good speed to you,' she added, shutting the door firmly in their faces.

Bemused, they gathered up their things, loaded the horses and set off.

Fleabag jumped onto Porridge with Gemma. 'Something is very wrong here,' he said. 'You've seen how miserable and frightened everyone is? Even the animals are in terror. Do you think we should turn back?'

Gemma shrugged. 'Well, *I* can't. You can do what you like.'

'If I was King,' muttered Phelan as a man pulled his child inside a house as they approached, 'I would put this place right first. Perhaps even before Rupertsberg. Something very strange is going on.'

They made the city of Beriot late that afternoon. Rowanne's money was beginning to run low, but she bought everyone a good meal and a night's lodging at an inn. 'This is my last treat,' she said. 'We will have to sleep rough after this—I have to keep the rest of my money to buy a swift horse to return next week.'

Soon the smell of hot pie and roast potatoes filled the little inn. Through the crowded room came a young boy pushing a wooden trolley laden with enough food for twice their company. With a great deal of difficulty he managed to elbow his way through to the travellers' table.

'Compliments of the management,' he said, with a worried look on his face.

Rowanne caught the lad in her iron grip. 'What do you mean, boy?'

'Nothing to pay, Ma'am. The landlord says so. Ow!'

Rowanne gripped him even tighter. 'Landlords don't give away food like this to complete strangers. What's happening?'

Just then she caught a glimpse of the fat landlord in his white apron peering into the room.

She let the boy go. 'That looks very nice indeed, thank you,' she said loudly. 'Will you bring me some pepper?'

The boy scurried off and returned quickly with a small earthenware pot.

As he put it in front of her, he whispered, 'Please, my Lady, go away, back where you came from. As soon as you've eaten...' When Rowanne tried to grab the child again, he slipped away like an eel in a stream.

Gemma could not eat, but sipped unhappily at her tankard of ginger ale. At last she said, 'I feel in my bones it will be dangerous to go on, but I simply can't do anything else. If anyone wants to turn back, I shan't think the worse of them.'

Rowanne bristled. 'We've been through all this. Can't we just eat in peace for once? Unless you would *rather* I went?' she added icily. 'Then you can find the Ring and keep it for yourself!'

Fleabag glared over the tabletop from his place on Phelan's knee. 'How *dare* you?' he spat. 'Watch her, Phelan, I don't trust that so-called knight the length of a fishbone.' Then he ducked down under the table again and measured how far he would have to spring to catch Rowanne's knee with a particularly well-sharpened claw he had been nurturing just in case . . .

Phelan bent down and spoke softly in Fleabag's ear. 'Forget Rowanne for the moment. She's just frightened, like the rest of us. Would you go and slip into the kitchen and see what the local cats say about these people? I've got a funny feeling and I don't like it. I wouldn't desert Gemma for the world—as long as she says we're going the right way, I'm there beside her—but I'd like to know what we're walking into.'

Fleabag slid with a black silken smoothness from Phelan's knee, but before he could emerge from under the table, the inn door swung heavily open and a troop of soldiers marched into the room in rigid formation. The sergeant, a tall, dark-haired man in immaculate bright blue uniform and sporting a huge moustache thumped the bar and roared: 'Well, are there any volunteers this year?'

The travellers looked around in astonishment. But apart from themselves and the soldiers, the room was suddenly quite empty.

30

Prison!

The prison was extremely cold and depressing. The perpetual drip, drip, drip of fetid water seeping from the ceiling of the vault combined with the musty smells of rotting hay and stale urine. But the worst of it was not knowing why they were there or if they would get out. So much seemed to depend on their freedom, yet how could they explain it to anyone? Who would believe them anyway?

All night long they sat in a huddle and wondered if they had been wrong all along. Gemma felt guilty because she had brought her trusting friends so far on the say-so of a voice in her head.

Rowanne felt she should have been able to prevent their arrest if she had had her sword in her hand.

Phelan worried whether someone had recognized him from his thieving days and they had all been arrested on suspicion of being like-minded criminals.

The only faintly happy one amongst them was Fleabag who was having excellent sport with a family of rats and had killed three of them in less than an hour.

The night was long, dark and frightening.

At dawn, bolts were drawn back on the cell door. Then came a screeching, grating sound of keys in an ancient lock. The door opened slowly and heavy footsteps heralded a thickset, bald man with no teeth.

He kicked the door shut behind him and put a loaf and a jug of water on the floor, right where the drip from the ceiling landed.

The man straightened and grinned. 'So you're the volunteers. Well done. Most public-spirited of you, I must say! Congratulations! I hope you have a nice time at the festival.'

Phelan struggled to his feet with difficulty, because of the weight of iron manacles on his wrists. 'What is happening? Volunteers for what? Why are we here when we haven't done anything wrong?'

Rowanne also tried to get to her feet, but her chain was too short. 'I demand you tell us what's happening. I am the Lady Rowanne de Montiland of the Queen's Guard. You must release me and my companions immediately!'

The gaoler grinned and bowed. 'Pleased to meet you, I'm sure, my Lady. Now I'm sorry, I must go and see to the other lords and ladies in my care. "So much to do, so little time," as they say.'

As he was about to go out of the door he caught sight of Fleabag's hunting trophies. The man's face lit up and before the cat could move, he had caught Fleabag up and tucked him under his arm. 'Now you are what I call a useful sort of a cat. I'll keep you. He won't get *you*, no, he won't, puss.'

To everyone's amazement, Fleabag did not protest, but purred and snuggled up to his new master. The key turned in the lock and they were alone again.

Gemma sniffed and wiped her nose on her sleeve.

Phelan said quietly, 'Fleabag would never desert us. He probably thinks he may be able to help us best if he is free.'

'I'm sure you're right,' Gemma replied. 'It's just that it felt so awful to see him go off like that without even a lick goodbye.'

Rowanne started to examine her chains. 'If I had my dagger, I'm sure I could force one of these links,' she said. 'They're heavy but not particularly well made.'

'If I had a dagger I could pick the locks,' muttered Phelan. 'I'm quite good at that. In fact, I could probably do it with a hairpin . . .' He looked hopefully at Rowanne.

She rummaged under her woollen snood and pulled one out triumphantly. 'Will this do?'

'Perfect!' and he set to working on Rowanne's manacle. 'I'm starting with you because you're the best fighter. I'll do Gemma next because she is the most important. If you get a chance to run before I'm free, then go. And may the Ring Fire light your way.'

Gemma did not know what to say. She couldn't imagine running away without her friends.

For a long time Phelan worked in silence. The only sounds were the scratching of wire against iron and the dripping of water right onto their breakfast bread.

'Almost got it!' he whispered triumphantly at long last, but before he could snap the lock open, the thump of feet along the stone corridor made him drop the pin.

Seconds later, a sharp command halted a column of soldiers outside the door. The keys jangled again and the door swung reluctantly on its hinges.

The bald gaoler came and undid the chains. 'Time to go now, boys and girls,' he said cheerfully. 'You didn't eat the breakfast I cooked for you so loving-like. Tut, tut, that's a waste now, isn't it? Still, you won't need it where you're going.'

Next to him the sergeant barked, 'Get up!' and Gemma and Phelan found themselves jerked to their feet. Reluctantly Rowanne stood next to them and was about to demand her rights again, when she caught sight of Fleabag in the open doorway. He looked right through her, warning her to silence.

As they were marched out, he slipped between their feet unseen by the gaoler, who was left calling, 'Puss, puss? Nice bit o' fish I bin and bought for you. Here, puss!'

Fleabag skilfully matched his step with the soldiers and managed to leap into Gemma's arms. She buried her face in his warm fur. 'I'm scared, Fleabag.'

'So you should be,' replied the cat. 'I had a long talk with the gaoler's dog and I've found out what's going on.'

The prisoners were bundled into a covered wagon. Bars were put up to prevent their escape, and a thick oil cloth was thrown over so they could see nothing of the outside. The wagon began to move and they could hear the iron-clad wheels clattering over cobbles. Soon the noise gave way to a softer sound. 'Mud,' said Rowanne. 'We're out in the country again.'

Gemma put Fleabag down and he wriggled to the middle where they all could hear him. 'Now, this is what I have found out. It seems that there is a beast in these parts—I don't know what it is exactly, but many years ago it used to devour all the sheep and cattle for miles around. It is said it was lured into the depths of an ancient cavern and chained there. But by evil magic it slowly began to regain its strength. A few years ago it broke out and returned to its old ways.

'The Prince of this province pleaded with it to go away, but it would only do so if it was given humans to eat instead. However, in return, it now only feeds once a year—at the beginning of the Spring Festival. It is also content with less, usually only one adult or two or three children. The people of this land seem to prefer this to having all their cattle and crops ruined at the beast's whim. Apparently more people used to die from simply being in the beast's way, than by the annual meal.

'That's terrible!' gasped Rowanne. 'Let me at it with a good sword and I will rid the land of this plague!'

'No good,' replied Fleabag. 'It is plated all over with scales like steel, greased so thickly with slime that no sword can catch in it, let alone pierce it. But let me finish before we plan.

'It seems that before the Spring Festival, lots are drawn to choose that year's victim. Many people have lost loved ones.'

'No wonder everyone is so sad,' said Gemma.

'But the worst of it is, if there are any strangers in the land, they are put at the top of the list. The people are not inhospitable, but obviously they want to protect their own friends and families.'

Phelan whistled quietly. 'So we walked right into it. It all makes sense now.'

A strangled silence filled the wagon. Suddenly the friends were thrown together as it jerked to a halt. Fleabag hid himself under Gemma's cloak.

The black oilcloth was pulled back and dazzling daylight streamed in. Guards in blue uniforms tugged at the iron bars and tail-board until the trio fell back with a clatter. 'Out!' ordered the sergeant. 'Quick about it.'

They found themselves outside a small grey stone building with tiny, high windows. Phelan's heart sank, for to one side there were carpenters, busily constructing what could only have been a scaffold.

Phelan did not have long to look before he was pushed and shoved through a dark doorway and down steps. Once more they were in prison.

The room was small and square. Food, water and a bucket had been left for them. In the corner was a pile of blankets. Gemma handed one to everyone then wrapping herself up, she curled up in a corner.

Phelan came and sat next to her. 'We're not dead yet,' he said gently. 'Show us the Ring Fire, Gemma. We all need it.'

She opened her hands, though they were trembling.

There was no flame!

There was little time to think about their predicament, for the door opened again almost immediately.

'Which one of you is the Lady de something?' demanded the sergeant's stern, military voice.

Rowanne jumped to her feet. 'I am the Lady Rowanne de Montiland, and I demand to see your Prince.'

The man looked her up and down. 'I don't know about you seeing *him*, but he'll see *you*. You're first. Tomorrow at dawn.'

The man looked at the others. 'If the beast goes away after that, the rest of you will be free. If he doesn't, it'll be you, then you,' he jerked a thumb at Phelan and Gemma in turn. Then he looked down at Fleabag. 'We'll even use the cat if we have to.' He turned his sad face to Rowanne again. 'Because if he's not full after that, the lot has fallen on my little son.'

He turned smartly on his heel and left, slamming the door behind him.

Gemma lifted her head from her blanket. 'Once the old Queen told me that there had not been a dragon in the land for a hundred years. I wonder if it's the same one and people only thought it was dead.'

'I bet she became Queen because she was the one who got rid of it for them,' said Fleabag. 'It's just the sort of thing she would have done.'

Just then, Rowanne was violently sick in the bucket.

After a few moments she lifted her head. 'It's funny,' she said at last, 'but before a battle I'm nervous but never frightened. I've never known what it means to be really frightened before. I . . . I think it's because this time I have no weapons in my hands. Before, I always had my sword and my skills—it was an even match, if you like. But the thought of being chained up . . . out there, just waiting . . . I can't stand it.' And she collapsed into hysterical sobbing.

The others sat in silence, just watching and listening. There seemed to be nothing left to say.

31

A Bad Night

Whether Rowanne was asleep, or lying in a terrified stupor, Gemma did not know. But the grey shape against the opposite wall did not move all night.

Gemma did not sleep either. She would have welcomed oblivion for a few hours to make the inevitable come more quickly, but she was too cold. A few hours before dawn, Phelan pushed his old jacket over to her.

'Take it,' he whispered. 'I don't feel the cold as badly as you do.'

Gemma pulled the coat over her shoulders and leaned back. But sleep still did not come. She was almost warm enough now, but there was an uncomfortable lump against her back and, however she twisted, she could not shift it.

At last, Fleabag who had been asleep on her lap, got up in disgust. 'A cat's got to get beauty sleep!' he moaned. 'Even a condemned cat.' And he curled up under the table.

Soon the dull blue-grey of first light began to creep into the cell from a small grating above their heads. Phelan stood and went over to Rowanne. Gently he pulled the blanket back from her face, then let it drop again.

He sat down next to Gemma.

'Are you awake?'

'Yes.'

'I'm going to take Rowanne's place. I'm sure the beast won't care whether he gets a knight or a thief. I'm taller than her and there's a chance I might fill him up better.'

Gemma looked at him with wide eyes. She did not know what to say.

'Rowanne can't do it. I have never seen anyone look as terrified as she does. If I go, it gives you three another full day to think of a way out of this mess.' Phelan held out his hand to Gemma. 'Goodbye. Thanks for everything.'

Gemma shook his hand.

At last she managed to find her voice. 'But you've always been frightened of beasts—wolves and things . . . And the scaffold was your worst nightmare because of the way your parents died!'

'That was dread—it eats into you so you can't function any more. It's funny, but the dread has gone away quite suddenly. Now I'm just scared. That's different. I'm not being brave. It's just that I've got to do it—Rowanne can't. And I keep thinking about the other people, like that soldier's boy, who will be next. I might at least be able to give them another year.

'All I ask is that you'll take any chance to escape. Don't martyr yourself in memory of me or anything stupid. You of all people must get back. Who knows what crook or tyrant may be holding the Ring at this very moment? You must be sure the holder is a true king or queen. And Rowanne—she must get back too. She must speak for the people who are suffering across the land. So run the second you can. Promise?'

'I promise.'

Phelan hesitated. 'I've got two more favours to ask.'

'Anything.'

'Will you light a little of the Ring Fire for me when I'm out there? It will help me go through with it.'

'If the Fire will burn at all, I will burn it until I drop, like the Fire Wielder.'

'... And the last thing...'

'Yes?'

'Can I have my coat back? I'm freezing.'

Gemma laughed, although she wanted to cry. She pulled the jacket from around her shoulders and passed it across to him. 'There's a funny lump in the lining at the back. It kept me awake all night.'

Just then the sound of footsteps echoed along the passageway. 'Light the Fire now,' whispered Phelan. He watched the tiny glow glimmering between her fingers, then he stood to attention next to the door, waiting for the moment it would open.

32

The Wolf Prince

On the first morning of the Spring Festival every man, woman, child and animal was safely barricaded in cellars and basements. No one moved or even breathed lest the beast should come their way.

The stench of its breath was beginning to seep under doors and through loose windowframes. Dawn had come, but a thick cloud hovered across the face of the sun. Slowly the cloud grew blacker and denser, until at last it took the shape of a serpent-like creature with blood-red scales and two pairs of huge leathery wings, beating the air with a singeing, searing heat.

The land was empty. There was no one to see the monster approaching except the tiny figure of Phelan, chained to his scaffolding, and Prince Tomas of Beulothin, watching from one of the upper windows of the prison. The Prince was a thin, grey old man, dressed in funereal black and unashamedly weeping to see yet another victim go to his death. In the last few years the beast had been taking more and more people. Would there be enough prisoners in the dungeon to satisfy it this year?

He knew in his heart that one day there would not. On that day he must at last take off his crown and step forward himself to prevent the whole land being laid to waste.

The Prince was not cruel in letting the others go first. He was just scared—like everyone else.

As Phelan waited, the Ring Fire burned in Gemma's hands. Suddenly Gemma realized she could see pictures in the flames, just as she had done in the Queen's Ring all those long months ago. Of course—it was Phelan and Rowanne she had seen!

But now she saw only Phelan, chained and alone. Suddenly she wished she had given him a tiny flame, to comfort him. But perhaps that couldn't be done. It was too late now, anyway.

The monster had landed. It scraped its rattling metallic scales across the fields, leaving the stench of burning slime behind it.

Slowly it approached the scaffold, snarling and glaring hungrily at Phelan. But it did not attack straight away. It seemed to be considering its prey.

Gemma held her breath. She was concentrating on Phelan so hard that there was no room for any-thing else, even her fear. Suddenly she realized that, for the first time, the Ring Fire was burning *inside* her. She had become one with it, and was surround-ing Phelan with the Fire glow.

She saw him standing straight and still, but she could feel dread pulsing all around him. 'Don't let the dread come back,' she whispered. 'Or you won't be able to think.'

'No,' she heard him say. 'I must be able to think.'

Then he did a strange thing. He seemed to be rummaging in his coat pocket.

At last he pulled out something small and knobbly. He held it in his hand and watched the beast approaching. It had stopped in front of him, sniffing and flicking its lurid green tongue as it stretched its sagging neck towards its prey . . .

Gemma held the picture of Phelan surrounded by the Ring Fire. She dare not let it waver for one moment. His dread must not return.

Phelan seemed to be measuring the distance. Waiting. Calculating.

Suddenly the beast opened its maw and engulfed its victim in a cloud of asphyxiating smoke. Phelan choked and retched, but he swung back his arm and threw the small knob right into the cavernous mouth.

The creature swallowed it and looked surprised. Then it flung back its head to roar. But the noise caught in its throat. It looked down at Phelan and opened its mouth again. But this time, scalding black blood belched out.

The beast swung its head from left to right as if it was in agony. It arched its back high and crashed down onto the scaffold, splintering it from end to end.

Phelan was left hanging like a puppet in his chains.

But still the beast did not attack. Instead it writhed and flung its huge body from side to side, rolling and crashing until it finally lay on one side, lashing its tail and howling with a terrible bellow that echoed in all the hills for miles around.

After what seemed an eternity the steam and stench subsided and the creature lay quite still.

A word from the Prince, and soldiers swarmed onto the field. They all drew their swords and tried to hack the beast's head off, but to no avail.

Then Prince Tomas himself was at Phelan's side unlocking the chains that bound him.

Phelan was dazed and sick. Dizzily he sank to the ground and sat staring at the body of the beast.

'Deathcap.'

'What?' asked the Prince.

'Deathcap toadstool. I lost one in the lining of my coat months ago, but I found it this morning. I thought that if the beast could not be killed from the *outside*, than perhaps I could kill it from the *inside*.'

He shook his head and whistled. 'I didn't realize the effects were *that* quick.' Then he grinned.

'Good job they were, though.'

And with that, he fainted.

Soldiers came and flung the prison door open. Gemma dashed out, with Fleabag hot on her heels. Daylight had never felt so real or so welcoming. The sun was beginning to come out again, as everywhere the poisonous blackness thinned and blew away in the morning breezes.

Gemma ran over to the beast's head and looked into its dead eyes. Carefully, she placed a flame of the Ring Fire onto the greasy head. Then she leaped back, for with a great roar of flame the whole creature caught light and began to burn.

When Phelan woke, he was in the Prince's own

bedroom in the palace at Beriot. Gemma and Rowanne were seated next to him. They had bathed and eaten well.

Fleabag had begged to be excused because he preferred his fish raw, and did not think the Prince's bedroom was quite the place to eat it.

'Try and eat something,' coaxed Gemma as soon as Phelan opened his eyes. 'There's no deathcap amongst the fried mushrooms. I've checked.'

Phelan grinned weakly and sat up. 'Ow! Why do I hurt so much?'

'You've got bad burns from the beast's breath, but you'll be all right,' Rowanne replied. 'But first of all, I want to thank you for doing what you did. I never realized I was such a coward before—or such a snob. To think I once wanted you hanged!'

Phelan shook his head. 'Each to his own. I'd be useless in battle. I just suddenly found my dread had gone, and I could meet the monster. I'd forgotten about the deathcap until the last minute. I don't know where I got the courage—or how I remembered the fungus.'

'Gemma kept the Ring Fire burning all the time,' Rowanne told him. 'She *willed* you through it.'

'I know. I could feel it. I think the real thanks go to you, Gemma.'

Gemma smiled. 'No, to the Ring Fire and the Fire Giver. Now eat up, someone wants to see you.'

Phelan ate a little, then a servant came and dressed him in a loose silk robe that would not chafe his burns. Painfully he eased himself into a chair and the door opened. In walked Prince Tomas himself, attended by all sixteen of his advisers.

As the Prince approached, he knelt and took off his crown. He handed it to Phelan.

'Twenty years ago, when the beast returned, I begged it to go. It told me it would leave for ever if I would let it take me. I thought it was a trick to get me to leave my land unprotected. I never told anyone, but I convinced myself I was needed to rule the province. Really, I was too frightened to dare to look death in the face, even for the sake of my people.'

'I am no longer fit to rule. In the name of our departed Queen, and whoever her successor may be, please be Prince of this province.'

Phelan stared at the Prince, and the crown that had been placed in his hands. He turned it over and looked at it. 'I—I don't know what to say . . . is this your will also?' he asked the advisers standing behind the Prince.

A tall dark-skinned woman stepped forward and bowed. 'Our Prince has served us well and faithfully for many years. But if he feels he must abdicate in favour of one who is braver and will serve his people better than himself, we can only agree. We vow to serve you as well as our skills permit.' She bowed again, and stepped back, pulling her emerald silk gown around her.

By this time, Fleabag had finished his supper and returned, licking his whiskers contentedly. 'Now there's an offer you can't refuse. The food here is first-rate. I'll stay and be your chief adviser if you like.'

Phelan laughed. Fleabag had given him a moment to make his mind up. 'Two wonderful offers,' he said. 'I am indeed a rich man! But I cannot accept, because we must leave very soon. My friends and I must return to Harflorum, for the year and the day is almost up when the Queen's successor will be presented. For many reasons we must be there.

'But more importantly, although I am deeply honoured, you must realize that just because I had an old toadstool in my pocket it does not mean that I would be a good prince. You understand your people. You know their needs. Please—keep your crown.'

Prince Tomas was not to be deterred. 'But I have *not* served my people faithfully. I am no prince at all.' He offered the crown again.

Phelan thought for a moment. 'If I accept, may I go away to complete my other tasks first?'

The advisers conferred for a few moments. 'Of course, Sir,' they agreed heartily.

'Then I accept,' Phelan said, inclining his head. 'But on condition that I have a good regent to rule in my place. Is this good in your eyes, my Lords and Ladies who advise the Prince?'

Again they agreed.

'Then, Prince Tomas of Beulothin, I appoint you as my regent.' And he leaned forward and placed the crown firmly back on the thin grey hair of the Prince. As he did so he whispered, 'You will be a much better prince from now on. You won't forget today, will you?'

'Never, my Lord.'

'Then get up. You have work to do.'

Prince Tomas no longer looked so grey and old. Years seemed to have fallen away from him. He smiled at all the company. 'We will have a banquet tonight in your honour. The people have many gifts to give to you. Please rest until then, my Lord and Ladies.'

'And Cat!' purred Fleabag from the place of honour he had claimed for himself on Phelan's lap.

The Prince bowed to Fleabag and left the room with all his counsellors in tow.

Gemma and Rowanne looked at each other and whistled.

'Well, I never,' said the cat. 'Prince Phelan—the Wolf Prince.'

'I'll present Rowanne with that catfur collar she's always wanted if you ever call me that again,' Phelan laughed, pretending to cuff the cat around the ear.

Then he looked at Gemma. Her face was long and miserable. 'What's the matter? Don't worry, I'll come back with you and then after that—who knows? But at least I always have a home and both of you are welcome to be part of it for as long as it pleases you. Gemma will never have to peel another potato as long as she lives—and Rowanne, what would you like? To be Captain of the Guard?'

Gemma shook her head. 'It's not that at all. It's just that I have this awful feeling that I have to go soon—very soon. I'm sure you'll think me terribly rude, but I can't help it—the Ring Fire is calling me. It's urgent. We may not have found the Ring, but I am needed.'

Phelan looked from the cat to the knight, then back to Gemma again. 'You're right. I feel it too.'

Fleabag jumped down from Phelan's lap. 'Shame,' he said. 'The dustbins here are superb.'

33

Return to Harflorum

The hours before the banquet were very busy with preparations for the journey. Prince Tomas gave Rowanne and Phelan good horses and Gemma a sure-footed pony. Fleabag was given a special pannier where he could sleep like a king on a soft new fleece.

Supplies were packed onto the backs of three strong horses, but as time was of the essence, only two soldiers were sent to protect and speed the party on the road.

It was almost dark when everything was ready. Gemma wanted to ride through the night as soon as the banquet was over, but Rowanne persuaded her that the horses might stumble which would slow them badly. It had to be daylight travel as much as possible. On top of that, Phelan really needed a night's sleep; he was far from well after his encounter with the beast.

Fleabag permitted his fur to be washed and combed dry, then a scarlet silk ribbon was tied around his neck. He sat on a fat satin cushion at the end of the high table and held court with all the admiring palace cats.

Rowanne dressed in formal knightly dress. She wore white silk stockings and knee length breeches, with a loose lawn shirt and a cloth-of-gold tabard. Her short cloak was of scarlet satin edged with gold. For once she let her hair fall loose and tumbling down her back.

As she entered everyone gasped. Even Fleabag admitted that he had never quite thought of her as *beautiful* before.

Gemma had her hair cut properly. It had never looked right since 'Auntie' had hacked it in the thieves' kitchen. Now it was neat and shiny. Phelan had given orders that she should wear a long robe of flame-red silk. Gemma did not think it was really her colour, but she did not like to turn it down.

Phelan himself would only wear a plain white linen shirt and trousers, with a blue woollen waist-coat. He too had his black hair and beard cut short, so it curled tightly around his dark face. To please Prince Tomas, he wore the small golden crown of the princedom, but he took it off again as soon as he politely could, on the pretext that it kept slipping to one side.

The four travellers looked at each other in amazement. None of them would have recognized the others, they were so transformed. Phelan took Rowanne and Gemma in to dinner, one on each arm, and they were seated at the High Table.

After the food and the speeches there was dancing and merriment. The whole city was alive with music and fireworks. Flashes of bonfires and squeals from rockets brought the night sky to life all the way across the province.

At last Gemma felt she really *had* to go to bed. She wanted to be on the road at dawn and there was little enough time left for sleep as it was.

As Phelan went to follow the others to the sleeping chambers, the Prince caught him by the arm.

'We must give you our gifts,' insisted the Prince. 'All the people have bought you tokens of their gratitude.'

'But apart from making me a prince you have given us these beautiful clothes and equipped us for our return. That is more than enough,' protested Phelan.

'No, no, not a bit of it,' laughed the Prince. And he led him into another room which was piled high with boxes and packages of every conceivable shape and size.

Phelan blanched. 'I can't possibly... I mean, what would we *do* with it all?' he muttered.

'Please,' begged the Prince, 'take *something* as a token of our love and gratitude, otherwise the people will be offended.'

Phelan sighed. 'I will take one small thing as a token. My friends may also take what they will, but I beg you, take everything that is here and give it to the poor in the land. There is more here than any man could even *look at* in one lifetime—let alone *possess*.

'Show me where the smallest gifts are to be found, for I cannot take anything bulky with me.'

A servant led Phelan to a table at the back of the room, where blue and purple velvet cases containing the rarest jewels of the Kingdom were laid out. He walked past them with barely a glance. At the very end, tucked almost out of sight, lay a little olive-wood box carved with the symbol of the Ring Fire on its lid.

'What is this?' he picked it up and turned it over.

'I do not know, Sir,' replied the servant. 'None of us has been able to open it. Maybe it is just a carving. It is nothing.' He shrugged.

Phelan smiled. 'Then I will take it. It is very small and light and it will fit easily into my pocket. It will remind me that it is only the Ring Fire which has brought me here. Thank you.' And with that he bowed to the Prince and went to bed.

As the first light softened the black curves of the countryside, Gemma was up and dressed in new travelling clothes. They were very much like her old ones but warmer and with no holes. The Queen's shoes still fitted her, but they leaked terribly, so she had them packed with her other gear as she could not bear to be parted from them.

Rowanne appeared at her door. She too had fresh riding clothes but best of all, she had a bright sword slung at her side and a finely wrought new dagger. 'Personal gifts from Phelan,' she grinned. 'I think we're even now.' Then she caught sight of Fleabag, who had made a special effort to get his fur comfortably matted again.

'Don't look at me,' he said. 'You'll never have my hide round your neck. I've acquired some particularly itchy fleas here. Would you like one?'

Prince Tomas waved the friends off, but there were no lengthy farewells; Gemma's sense of urgency would not permit it. Rowanne was a little grumpy. She was greatly enjoying the fuss that was made of her and would have liked to spend time in the Prince's stables and working out with one or two of his knights in the practice yard. Her sword-fighting had really become rusty of late and she doubted if she could still unhorse an opponent with a lance.

She looked longingly at the archery butts as the horses wheeled out of the yard, but then she turned her attention south by south-east.

Day after day, they rode with the sun in their eyes all morning. The soldiers accompanying them set up strong canvas tents at night, so no time was lost looking for accommodation, except when the spring rains came. Then they were forced to stop in a small village as floods swept across the low-lying ground and cut them off for a whole week.

Gemma fretted and wouldn't eat. She sat morosely looking out of the upstairs window of the cottage where they were staying and watched the waters swirl endlessly.

Rowanne champed at the bit. She paced up and down the short muddy street asking every inhabitant how long the floods usually lasted and how deep the draining ditches were. She drew up calendar after calendar, deciding that each one must be wrong. They had left several days before the equinox, but every day was precious. At last, the tops of grass shoots appeared in rough patches here and there amongst the smooth yellow-grey flood water. The next day muddy banks appeared. Rowanne tried to find the road with her horse, but she could not locate the bridge they needed to cross the swirling submerged river.

Two days later they were on the road again.

Slowly the days lengthened and warmed until blossom and leaf filled the air with the rich smells of early summer. They had only a few days left when at last they reached Rupertsberg.

Rowanne reined in her horse and looked silently for several minutes. 'We must go round it. I must not even ride through, or we may never make it in time.' And with that she urged her chestnut stallion along the wide road that ran along the foot of the walls. With every bit of speed they could muster the party galloped up the next hill and through the wood where Phelan's gang had first attacked. But the ex-thief looked neither to his right nor to his left. He bowed his head over his horse's mane and rode.

The city of Harflorum was situated on a small hill overlooking wide plains which rolled to the south. The approach road from the north-west wound between hills and woods, then opened out suddenly on the view. Everywhere the scent of May blossom filled the air. Gardens were springing verdant with strong young seedlings. Everything looked peaceful.

Until they reached the gates.

The soldiers admitted the party as they were obviously visiting dignitaries, but everywhere the streets were crammed with people from every corner of the kingdom.

Everywhere stank of bodies pressed together. People jostled and crammed and pushed. Thieves plied their trade, as did pedlars with trays of imitation opal rings and fire jugglers breathing 'real Ring Fire' from their noses and mouths. Mothers struggled to get frightened children home through the crush. Everywhere was turmoil.

Gently, the friends eased their horses through the throng until they reached the palace gates. Rowanne leaned over and gave her name to a guard who did not know her.

'I don't care who you are, you take your place with the rest. The queue goes on right round the palace. Be patient and you'll get your turn.' And with that he turned her horse's head and slapped the animal on the flank. The frightened horse swung badly from left to right, but Rowanne controlled it with a tight rein.

'This is hopeless,' Rowanne yelled above the hubbub. She called to the guards who had accompanied them. 'Take the horses and find somewhere for yourselves to sleep outside the city. This is no place for the animals—nor for anyone who doesn't need to be here. We will send for you in a few days.'

The soldiers saluted and led the horses out of the city. Gemma kept close in behind Rowanne. The crush frightened her. Crowds always made her feel as if she could not breathe, but she must not faint this time. Fleabag jumped up onto Phelan's shoulder so he could be carried.

'What do we do now, clever-clogs?' the cat asked rudely.

Rowanne scowled at him. 'Why can't you be useful for a change? Jump down and see how we can get into the palace.'

The cat scrambled down, inadvertently scratching Phelan as he went. Swiftly he dodged the many feet and disappeared.

'What do we have to queue for, anyway?' asked Phelan out loud.

A short fat woman with a water bottle and a cup

was shoving her way through the masses. 'You want to know what this is all about? Don't you know? Goodness me!' she tutted, 'where have you been for the past year? These are all people who are wanting to show their opal rings to the Fire Wielder in case they have found the true Ring. Trouble is, he's very weak. He won't live much longer, and he's certainly too frail to see anyone, so we're all just sitting here. Only got to wait until tomorrow though, then the year and a day's up! I'm doing all right, though. Would you like to buy a drink, dearie?' she turned to Gemma.

'No, thank you. But what happens at the end of tomorrow if he still can't see anyone?'

The woman shrugged and her three chins wobbled. 'Dunno. There'll be a big fight, I suppose. I won't stick around for it, though.' She turned to the next person behind them. 'Buy a drink, dearie?'

Just then Fleabag came panting back and leapt into Phelan's arms again. He looked quite exhausted.

'I've found a way to get into the palace, if you don't mind going through the kitchen. Cook left the door ajar. But the bad news is he's there and in a filthy temper.'

Gemma winced at this, but Rowanne, who had heard all about Cook's ways, pulled herself up to her full height. 'Come on, cat!' she said, 'Let's have him for supper, shall we?'

Carefully they edged their way through the people, until they reached the wall of the kitchen garden. As Fleabag had said, the gate was slightly ajar. Phelan pushed it open and they all slipped inside.

Cook, who had been beating one of the kitchen boys, stopped and looked up at the intruders. He dropped the poor unfortunate lad into the sage bush and turned on the others, brandishing his rolling pin.

Fleabag took good aim and leapt with all fifteen claws splayed and caught Cook on the face. At the same moment Phelan wrested the rolling pin from his fist.

With a strong hold, Rowanne caught the greasy man's arm behind his back, and marched him along the path, opened the garden door and pushed him firmly outside so he fell right into the gutter.

Phelan pushed the door shut and locked it with a satisfied sigh. 'It'll be a long time before he's able to get back in *here!*' He grinned.

All the kitchen staff were crowded around the pantry door, watching with open mouths what had happened to the tyrant. As the travellers stepped into the kitchen, they were all applauded. Fleabag excused himself and went to have a quick look at his favourite dead rat, to see whether it was ready to eat after having matured behind Cook's chair for a whole year.

Gemma led the way from the back stairs where she and Fleabag used to talk. Without pausing they ran straight past the butler, who did not dare to stop them, and into the main hall. There they turned left and went up the next flight of stairs to the top of the palace. At the end of the next corridor was the Hall of Light.

There Gemma stood still.

'What are we going to *say?*' she asked, looking at the others with a worried frown. 'We have nothing to show him.'

34

The King and the
Fire Wielder

'Well, at least let's see him and tell him we tried,' said
the cat practically.

Gemma put her hand against the door and gave it
a gentle push.

'You can't go in there,' yelled a stentorian voice
from behind them.

Rowanne swung round. It was the Captain of the
Queen's Guard. She stood to attention and saluted
smartly. 'Sir!' she said, 'I have escorted this lady for
many miles at the Fire Wielder's request. I am sure
that he will want to see us.'

The Captain relaxed as he recognized Rowanne,
and said very quietly. 'I'm sorry. It's impossible.
Don't you know he's dying? It won't be much longer.'

'But he expressly ordered me...' began Rowanne.

While they were arguing, Fleabag pressed both
front paws on the heavy carved door and pushed it
open. 'Psst, leave them at it,' whispered the cat.
'Rowanne likes a good row—she'll be fine.'

The three of them crept into the Hall. Phelan stood uncertainly on the threshold, but Gemma beckoned him to follow. The room was silent, and filled with the soft light of an early summer evening.

Asleep on the *chaise longue*, apparently just as they had left him a year ago, lay the Fire Wielder. He had become very thin. His round face was sunken now and the once golden-brown skin was pale and sallow. His hooked nose looked huge against his wasted features. He seemed unutterably tired.

On the table next to him, burned a tiny, weak flame, not much bigger than a glowing match head. All that was left of the Ring Fire. 'I must have used it all up,' said Gemma. 'I do hope it's not too late.'

'Quick,' said Phelan. 'I hear more guards coming.'

At this, Fleabag jumped onto the Fire Wielder's chest and licked his face. 'Wake up, Sir,' he said. 'We're back!'

The old man moaned, opened his eyes and smiled. 'I had been dreaming you were on your way,' he said weakly. 'I hoped it was true. Now, give me the Ring. We will put the Fire back straight away.'

'We haven't got it, Sir,' Gemma said, hanging her head. 'Everything went wrong. Either that or I misheard. Anyway, I failed you and the Queen.'

'Nonsense!' snapped the old man, lifting his tired grey head from the pillow. He waved a finger at Phelan. 'You there, let's see what you've got tucked away.'

Bemused, Phelan pulled a penknife, some string, a candle end and the little carved wooden box from the depths of his trouser pocket. 'I've only got these and a dirty handkerchief.'

'Open that!' said the Fire Wielder, pointing to the little box.

Phelan was about to protest that it *wouldn't* open, when he noticed a narrow gap in the side. Carefully he eased the crack further apart and there, on a bed of sea-green velvet, lay the Queen's Ring.

'Give it here, boy. Gemma, pass me the Ring Fire. Gently, it is very faded.'

Gemma picked up the tiny flicker of flame. For one awful second she thought it had gone out, but it steadied between her fingers.

The Fire Wielder lifted his tired hands and tried to hold the Ring and the Fire, but he was too weak. His thin fingers fell uselessly back onto the quilt that covered him.

'You'll have to do it for me, child. Just let the Flame flow into the Ring. There, that's right! Now,' his voice had almost sunk to a whisper, 'put it on the boy's finger. What's your name, lad?'

'Phelan, Sir.'

'Phelan, do you swear to be a good King and to serve your people faithfully all your days?'

Phelan opened his mouth and looked aghast.

'Go on! Do you?' Fleabag prompted.

'Yes, Sir, I do.'

'Well, that's settled.' The old man let his head rest back in the pillow, but his bright eye held Gemma in its gaze. 'And you, Gemma by name, Gem by nature, do you swear to carry the Ring Fire so that Phelan here will always have light to see by as he rules the land?'

Gemma swallowed hard. '*Me*?' she gulped.

'Of course, child, you! Who else? You've carried the Ring Fire all year. No one else has had any practice at it. It's *got* to be you! Gemma Fire Wielder, the latest of our line. Carry it well.'

Phelan nudged her.

'Yes,' she replied quietly. 'I swear.'

'Even better,' he said, closing his eyes and smiling. 'That's everything seen to now.' And he went to sleep.

Gemma held the old man's hand and felt his breathing slow until it was scarcely a flicker in his chest.

'He won't waken again, I'm afraid,' Phelan said softly.

'But what happens now?' Gemma asked.

'I think you ought to speak to your visitors,' Fleabag interrupted. 'There's lots of them.'

With a jump, Gemma and Phelan turned to see the room was full of people, mostly court officials— the Prime Minister, the Captain of the Guard and, standing in front of them all, the Lady Knight Rowanne de Montiland.

Suddenly, the knight pulled her sword from its sheath and knelt before Phelan, offering the hilt to the young King.

'My Lord,' she said. 'In more ways than one, my life is yours.'

There was a murmur of steel and a rustle of clothes as one by one, everyone in the room followed suit. Gemma started to kneel as well, but Fleabag stopped her. 'Don't, you silly girl. *You're* the Fire Wielder. You hold the flame high for everyone to see.'

Gemma lifted one thin arm and let the Fire burn until it filled the evening-darkened room with a glorious light. When she looked around, even Phelan was kneeling.

'All homage to the Ring Fire,' the King said, 'in which we live and move and have our being.'

The next few hours were a blur to Gemma. Everyone wanted to make a fuss of her—especially the butler who had kicked her so viciously when she had been a mere kitchenmaid.

She and Phelan were taken away by lords- and ladies-in-waiting, bathed and dressed in the finest robes. Fleabag made himself scarce when a maid came in his direction with a flea comb.

The next day, Gemma looked ruefully out of the palace windows and watched the children playing in the gardens. At that moment she would have given anything to be with them, running free and scruffy across the grass.

When she saw the heavy red and gold embroidered over-garments she was expected to wear all the time, she winced and bit her lip. She remembered how hot and uncomfortable the old Fire Wielder had looked the first time they had met. Suddenly she turned to the servant who was dressing her.

'I'm not going to wear these,' she announced. 'I've been carrying the Ring Fire for a year and a day, and I never needed heavy robes—so I'm not going to start now.' With that she ran from the room and disappeared down the servants' stairs and into the garden.

As she ran she was grabbed by a dark figure who had been hiding behind a tangled rambling rose. It was a miserable-looking Phelan.

'This means the end of all our fun—all our freedom,' he said unhappily. 'You ought to see the *stuff* I'm expected to wear! And worse than that, they've been lecturing me on how a king is expected to behave—all those *rules*. I won't be able to stand it. I wish I'd known before I made my vow to the Fire Wielder. I would have said "no".'

Gemma squatted next to her friend. 'I know,' she replied. 'I feel exactly the same.' Then she shifted suddenly as she felt the rose thorns pricking her back. But it wasn't a rose. It was Fleabag.

'Who do you think made the rules in the first place?' the cat inquired. 'Who thought of all those silly clothes and stuffy rules?'

'Other kings and other Fire Wielders, I suppose.'

'So who would have the authority to *unmake* the rules?' Fleabag persisted.

Phelan sprang up and looked at Gemma with glee. 'Why, *us*, of course!' He grabbed her hands and swung her around three times until they tripped and fell into a dizzy, rolling tumble all the way down the steeply sloping lawn.

When at last they stopped, all muddied and grass-stained, they were met by wide-eyed children staring in amazement to see the King and the Fire Wielder acting in this way.

Within seconds the lords- and ladies-in-waiting came swooping down from the palace armed with sponges, towels and royal robes, all clicking their tongues.

'Oh, go away!' Phelan laughed. 'From now on, when we're not doing something important, we're just going to be ourselves!'

Gemma did agree to wear a heavy gold and red embroidered robe for the Fire Wielder's funeral, as a mark of respect for the office she held.

Solemnly she led the procession from the palace to the graveyard on the sunny slope behind the city. Although she was sad at having lost someone so special, she knew he was glad to be sleeping the Long Sleep. The old Fire Wielder had been so tired.

After the funeral was over she sent her servants away and just sat quietly stroking Fleabag, smoothing his silky fur between her fingers. He was as dear and as ugly as ever. He sprang into her lap and they cried together until a flame-red sunset burned the evening sky with livid fire.

It was there that Phelan found them. He had taken off his royal robes and told his attendants in no uncertain terms that he wished to be left alone.

He sat quietly with them until the crimson and gold sky faded to indigo. At last he stood up.

'It is over now,' he said gently. 'Tomorrow we have other things to think about.'

The coronation was not held in the great throne room—or anywhere in the palace. Phelan insisted that if he were to be King of the people, he must be crowned amongst them.

On the last day of June, when the sun shone most strongly, an ordinary wooden chair bedecked with scarlet and yellow ribbon was carried to a large field

FEWER EMERGENCIES

by **Martin Crimp**

Cast
Rachael Blake
Neil Dudgeon
Paul Hickey
Tanya Moodie

Director **James Macdonald**
Designer **Tom Pye**
Lighting Designer **Martin Richman**
Sound Designer **Ian Dickinson**
Music **Mel Mercier**
Casting **Lisa Makin**
Production Manager **Sue Bird**
Stage Managers **Rebecca Austin, Jemma Gardner**
Costume Supervisor **Jackie Orton**
Company Voice Work **Patsy Rodenburg**
Set Construction **FIwFI**

THE COMPANY

Martin Crimp (writer)
For the Royal Court: Advice to Iraqi Women
(2003), Face to the Wall (2002),
The Country (2000), Attempts on Her Life (1997),
The Treatment (1993), No One Sees the Video
(1991).
Other plays include: Cruel and Tender (Young Vic/
Vienna Festival, 2004); The Misanthrope (Young Vic,
1996); Getting Attention (West Yorkshire
Playhouse, 1992); Play with Repeats, Dealing with
Clair, Four Attempted Acts (Orange Tree Theatre,
1984-9).
Translations for the Royal Court: The Chairs (with
Theatre de Complicite, 1997).
Other translations include works by Genet,
Marivaux and Koltes for the Almeida, RSC, RNT
and Young Vic theatres.
Resident Dramatist at the Royal Court 1997.

Rachael Blake
Theatre includes: The Harletts (Cabaret); The Sacred
(Griffin Theatre); The Censor (Stables Theatre).
Television includes: Auf Wiedershen Pet, Grass
Root II, The Three Stooges, Nowhere to Land,
Good News Week, Wildside, Water Rats, Home
and Away, Corrigan, Fire II, Pacific Drive,
Heartbreak High.
Film includes: Derailed, Tom White, Perfect
Strangers, Whispering in the Dark, Lantana, Blind
Man's Bluff, Paws, Knock Knock.
Awards include: AFI Best Actress in a series, TV
Week Logie Most Outstanding Actress Award (for
Wildside); If Magazine Best Actress in a Film Award,
AFI Award for Best Actress in a feature film (for
Lantana); The Centenary Medal for services to the
Australian film industry, 2004 Best Actress Award
at the 24th Oporto International Film Festival,
Portugal, Best Actress at the Vladivostok Film
Festival (for Perfect Strangers).

Ian Dickinson (sound designer)
For the Royal Court: Way To Heaven, The Woman
Before, Stoning Mary (& Drum Theatre, Plymouth),
Breathing Corpses, Wild East, Shining City (& Gate,
Dublin), Lucky Dog, Blest Be the Tie (with Talawa
TC), Ladybird, Notes on Falling Leaves, Loyal
Women, The Sugar Syndrome, Blood, Playing the
Victim (with Told By an Idiot), Fallout, Flesh Wound,
Hitchcock Blonde (& Lyric), Black Milk,
Crazyblackmuthafuckin'self, Caryl Churchill Shorts,
Push Up, Fucking Games, Herons.
Other theatre includes: Port, As You Like It, Poor
Superman, Martin Yesterday, Fast Food, Coyote Ugly
(Royal Exchange, Manchester); Night of the Soul
(RSC/Barbican); Eyes of the Kappa (Gate); Crime &
Punishment in Dalston (Arcola); Search & Destroy
(New End); The Whore's Dream (RSC/Edinburgh).
Ian is Head of Sound at the Royal Court.

Neil Dudgeon
For the Royal Court: Mountain Language, Ashes to
Ashes, Blasted, Waiting Room Germany, Talking in
Tongues, Road, Shirley.
Other theatre includes: Closer, Yerma, School for
Wives (RNT); The Importance of Being Earnest,
Richard II (Royal Exchange, Manchester); The
Crackwalker (Gate); Miss Julie (Oldham Coliseum);
The Next Best Thing (Nuffield); The Daughter-in-
Law (Bristol Old Vic); A Collier's Friday Night
(Greenwich): The Changeling, School for Scandal
(Cambridge Theatre Co).
Television includes: The Return of Sherlock
Holmes, The Plan Man, Murder in Mind, Messiah I, II
III and IV, Dirty Tricks, Mrs Bradley Mysteries, Four
Fathers, Tom Jones, The Gift, Our Boy, Breakout,
Out of the Blue, The All New Alexi Sayle Show,
Common as Muck, Fatherland, Touch of Frost,
Sharpe's Eagles, Nice Town, Between the Lines,
Resnick, Nightvoice.
Film includes: Chromophobia, Bridget Jones: The
Edge of Reason, Breathtaking, Crossing the Border,
Revolver, Fools of Fortune, Red King White Knight,
Prick Up Your Ears.

Paul Hickey
For the Royal Court: Crazyblackmuthafuckin'self.
Other theatre includes: Playboy of the Western
World, Peer Gynt, Romeo and Juliet (RNT);
Protestants (Traverse/Soho); Dealer's Choice, My
Night With Reg (Birmingham Rep); The Merchant
of Venice (RSC); Pentecost (Donmar/Kennedy
Centre, Washington); Drink, Dance, Laugh, Lie
(Bush Theatre); In A Little World Of Our Own
(Donmar); The Deep Blue Sea (Royal Exchange);
Red Roses And Petrol, Lady Windermere's Fan, The
Ash Fire (Tricycle); Howling Moon Silent Sons, The
Plough and the Stars, The Silver Tassie, Aristrocrats
(Abbey Theatre); Spokesong Shiver (Rough Magic).
Television includes: Inspector Lynley, Poliakoff -Film
I, Murder Squad, Rebel Heart, Father Ted, The
Informant, The Governor, Nighthawks.
Film includes: Though the Sky Falls, Nora, Ordinary
Decent Criminal, The General, The American, The
Matchmaker, Moll Flanders, On the Edge, Saving
Private Ryan.

James Macdonald (director)
James has been Associate Director of the Royal
Court since 1992. He is currently on a NESTA
Fellowship.
For the Royal Court: Lucky Dog, Blood, Blasted,
4.48 Psychosis, Hard Fruit, Real Classy Affair,
Cleansed, Bailegangaire, Harry and Me, The
Changing Room, Simpatico, Blasted, Peaches,
Thyestes, The Terrible Voice of Satan, Hammett's
Apprentice, Putting Two and Two Together.
Other theatre includes: A Number (New York
Theatre Workshop); Troilus und Cressida, Die

Kopien (Berlin Schaubühne); 4.48 Psychose (Vienna Burgtheater); The Tempest, Roberto Zucco (RSC); The Triumph of Love (Almeida); Love's Labour's Lost, Richard II (Royal Exchange, Manchester); The Rivals (Nottingham Playhouse); The Crackwalker (Gate); The Seagull (Sheffield Crucible); Miss Julie (Oldham Coliseum); Juno and the Paycock, Ice Cream and Hot Fudge, Romeo and Juliet, Fool for Love, Savage/Love, Master Harold and the Boys (Contact Theatre); Prem (BAC/Soho Poly).
Opera includes: Eugene Onegin, Rigoletto (WNO); Die Zauberflöte (Garsington); Wolf Club Village, Night Banquet (Almeida Opera); Oedipus Rex, Survivor from Warsaw (Royal Exchange/Hallé); Lives of the Great Poisoners (Second Stride).

Mel Mercier (music)
Mel is a well-known performer on the Irish traditional instruments, the Bodhran and Bones. He has performed and collaborated extensively with pianist and composer Mícheál Ó Súilleabháin, and with John Cage and the Merce Cunningham Dance Company,
Music composition for theatre includes: Medea (Abbey/West End/Broadway/Paris/Rome); The Powerbook (RNT/Paris/Rome); Julius Caesar (Barbican/Paris/Madrid/Luxembourg); The Merchant of Venice, A Midsummer Night's Dream (Corcadorca, co-composed with Linda Buckley). Commissions include: Telephone and Gongs (2004), Kelly and Andy (2005), both for UCC Gamelan Ensemble; Panarama (Signature Music for Cork 2005: European Capital of Culture).
Mel is a lecturer in Music at University College Cork and specialises in Irish traditional music, Ethnomusicology, Javanese Gamelan, Indian classical music and Ewe Dance Drumming (Ghana).

Tanya Moodie
For the Royal Court: Incomplete and Random Acts of Kindness.
Theatre includes: A Doll's House, Medea (West Yorkshire Playhouse); Much Ado About Nothing (Salisbury Playhouse); The Vagina Monologues (Arts Theatre/UK tour); Anything Goes (GPO); The Prince of Homburg (RSC/Lyric, Hammersmith); Le Costume (Peter Brook's CICT); The Darker Face of Earth, The Oedipus Plays (RNT); The School for Scandal, Peer Gynt, Coriolanus, Measure for Measure (RSC); As You Like It (Bristol); The Piano Lesson (Tricycle).
Television includes: Archangel, Shane, Absolute Power, Prime Suspect, Promoted to Glory, In Deep, The Queen's Nose, High Stakes, Holby City, Always and Everyone, The Bill, Dr Willoughby, Maisie Raine, Boyz Unlimited, A Respectable Trade, Neverwhere, So Haunt Me, The Man From Auntie.
Film includes: Rabbit Fever, The Tulse Luper Suitcases, The Final Passage.

Tom Pye (designer)
Theatre includes: Powerbook (RNT); Turn of the Screw (Royal Opera); St. John Passion, Diary of One Who Vanished (ENO); Magic Flute (Opera North); Provence Fest, Don Giovanni (Peter Brook).
Theatre, New York includes: Medea (Fiona Shaw), The Angel Project (Lincoln Center Festival).
Design and art direction for film and television includes: Emmy-winning Gloriana, Richard II, Twelfth Night, Helen West, Just William, Late Michael Clark, Christie Malry's Own Double Entry.

Martin Richman (lighting designer)
Solo Exhibitions include: Frazzle (The Power House); Come to Light (Rhodes+Mann); Light and Space (Homer Gallery, New York City); Lucent (Dominic Berning); Priming Vision (Damasquine Gallery, Brussels).
Selected Exhibitions include: Underdesign (Jousse Enterprise, Paris); The Bombay Sapphire Blue Room; Light Proof (Venice); Psychedelia (Aeroplastics Gallery, Brussels); Chora (Underwood Street); Fused (Riba); New Art '96 (Barcelona.
Commissions/Projects include: Soho Hotel, Hampstead Theatre, Tyeseley Energy From Waste Facility (Birmingham); Wolverhampton Art Gallery; Wajs House (Brussels); Millennium Beacons (Bristol); Le Soir (Brussels); Landing Lights (Harton Staithes Ferry, South Shields); The Women's Library (Whitechapel); Spiraline (Derby Playhouse); Float (Canary Wharf); Dan Burt Residence (Maine, USA); Barts and the London NHS Trust; Phillip and Wendy Press Residence, London; Chambre de Commerce et D'Industrie du Havre (France); Peabody Estates (Silvertown, London); All Souls Church (Portland Place, London).
Awards include: RSA Art for Architecture Award 1995, National Lighting Design Awards 2000; RSA Art for Architecture Award 2000; RIBA Award 2003; American Institute of Architecture 2004; Civic Trust Award 2004; National Lighting Design Awards 2001; Royal Institute of Architecture of Ireland Award, RIBA Award.

THE ENGLISH STAGE COMPANY AT THE ROYAL COURT

The English Stage Company at the Royal Court opened in 1956 as a subsidised theatre producing new British plays, international plays and some classical revivals.

The first artistic director George Devine aimed to create a writers' theatre, 'a place where the dramatist is acknowledged as the fundamental creative force in the theatre and where the play is more important than the actors, the director, the designer'. The urgent need was to find a contemporary style in which the play, the acting, direction and design are all combined. He believed that 'the battle will be a long one to continue to create the right conditions for writers to work in'.

photo: Andy Chopping

Devine aimed to discover 'hard-hitting, uncompromising writers whose plays are stimulating, provocative and exciting'. The Royal Court production of John Osborne's Look Back in Anger in May 1956 is now seen as the decisive starting point of modern British drama and the policy created a new generation of British playwrights. The first wave included John Osborne, Arnold Wesker, John Arden, Ann Jellicoe, N F Simpson and Edward Bond. Early seasons included new international plays by Bertolt Brecht, Eugène Ionesco, Samuel Beckett, Jean-Paul Sartre and Marguerite Duras.

The theatre started with the 400-seat proscenium arch Theatre Downstairs, and in 1969 opened a second theatre, the 60-seat studio Theatre Upstairs. Some productions transfer to the West End, such as Terry Johnson's Hitchcock Blonde, Caryl Churchill's Far Away and Conor McPherson's The Weir. Recent touring productions include Sarah Kane's 4.48 Psychosis (US tour) and Ché Walker's Flesh Wound (Galway Arts Festival). The Royal Court also co-produces plays which transfer to the West End or tour internationally, such as Conor McPherson's Shining City (with Gate Theatre, Dublin), Sebastian Barry's The Steward of Christendom and Mark Ravenhill's Shopping and Fucking (with Out of Joint), Martin McDonagh's The Beauty Queen Of Leenane (with Druid), Ayub Khan Din's East is East (with Tamasha).

Since 1994 the Royal Court's artistic policy has again been vigorously directed to finding and producing a new generation of playwrights. The writers include Joe Penhall, Rebecca Prichard, Michael Wynne, Nick Grosso, Judy Upton, Meredith Oakes, Sarah Kane, Anthony Neilson, Judith Johnson, James Stock, Jez Butterworth, Marina Carr, Phyllis Nagy, Simon Block, Martin McDonagh, Mark Ravenhill, Ayub Khan Din, Tamantha Hammerschlag, Jess Walters, Ché Walker, Conor McPherson, Simon Stephens, Richard Bean, Roy Williams, Gary Mitchell, Mick Mahoney, Rebecca Gilman, Christopher Shinn, Kia Corthron, David Gieselmann, Marius von Mayenburg, David Eldridge, Leo Butler, Zinnie Harris, Grae Cleugh, Roland Schimmelpfennig, Chloe Moss, DeObia Oparei, Enda Walsh, Vassily Sigarev, the Presnyakov Brothers, Marcos Barbosa, Lucy Prebble, John Donnelly, Clare Pollard, Robin French, Elyzabeth Gregory Wilder, Rob Evans, Laura Wade and Debbie Tucker Green. This expanded programme of new plays has been made possible through the support of A.S.K. Theater Projects and the Skirball Foundation, The Jerwood Charity, the American Friends of the Royal Court Theatre and (in 1994/5 and 1999) in association with the National Theatre Studio.

In recent years there have been record-breaking productions at the box office, with capacity houses for Joe Penhall's Dumb Show, Conor McPherson's Shining City, Roy Williams' Fallout and Terry Johnson's Hitchcock Blonde.

The refurbished theatre in Sloane Square opened in February 2000, with a policy still inspired by the first artistic director George Devine. The Royal Court is an international theatre for new plays and new playwrights, and the work shapes contemporary drama in Britain and overseas.

AWARDS FOR ROYAL COURT

Jez Butterworth won the 1995 George Devine Award, the Writers' Guild New Writer of the Year Award, the Evening Standard Award for Most Promising Playwright and the Olivier Award for Best Comedy for Mojo.

The Royal Court was the overall winner of the 1995 Prudential Award for the Arts for creativity, excellence, innovation and accessibility. The Royal Court Theatre Upstairs won the 1995 Peter Brook Empty Space Award for innovation and excellence in theatre.

Michael Wynne won the 1996 Meyer-Whitworth Award for The Knocky. Martin McDonagh won the 1996 George Devine Award, the 1996 Writers' Guild Best Fringe Play Award, the 1996 Critics' Circle Award and the 1996 Evening Standard Award for Most Promising Playwright for The Beauty Queen of Leenane. Marina Carr won the 19th Susan Smith Blackburn Prize (1996/7) for Portia Coughlan. Conor McPherson won the 1997 George Devine Award, the 1997 Critics' Circle Award and the 1997 Evening Standard Award for Most Promising Playwright for The Weir. Ayub Khan Din won the 1997 Writers' Guild Awards for Best West End Play and New Writer of the Year and the 1996 John Whiting Award for East is East (co-production with Tamasha).

Martin McDonagh's The Beauty Queen of Leenane (co-production with Druid Theatre Company) won four 1998 Tony Awards including Garry Hynes for Best Director. Eugene Ionesco's The Chairs (co-production with Theatre de Complicite) was nominated for six Tony awards. David Hare won the 1998 Time Out Live Award for Outstanding Achievement and six awards in New York including the Drama League, Drama Desk and New York Critics Circle Award for Via Dolorosa. Sarah Kane won the 1998 Arts Foundation Fellowship in Playwriting. Rebecca Prichard won the 1998 Critics' Circle Award for Most Promising Playwright for Yard Gal (co-production with Clean Break).

Conor McPherson won the 1999 Olivier Award for Best New Play for The Weir. The Royal Court won the 1999 ITI Award for Excellence in International Theatre. Sarah Kane's Cleansed was judged Best Foreign Language Play in 1999 by Theater Heute in Germany. Gary Mitchell won the 1999 Pearson Best Play Award for Trust. Rebecca Gilman was joint winner of the 1999 George Devine Award and won the 1999 Evening Standard Award for Most Promising Playwright for The Glory of Living.

In 1999, the Royal Court won the European theatre prize New Theatrical Realities, presented at Taormina Arte in Sicily, for its efforts in recent years in discovering and producing the work of young British dramatists.

Roy Williams and Gary Mitchell were joint winners of the George Devine Award 2000 for Most Promising Playwright for Lift Off and The Force of Change respectively. At the Barclays Theatre Awards 2000 presented by the TMA, Richard Wilson won the Best Director Award for David Gieselmann's Mr Kolpert and Jeremy Herbert won the Best Designer Award for Sarah Kane's 4.48 Psychosis. Gary Mitchell won the Evening Standard's Charles Wintour Award 2000 for Most Promising Playwright for The Force of Change. Stephen Jeffreys' I Just Stopped by to See the Man won an AT&T: On Stage Award 2000.

David Eldridge's Under the Blue Sky won the Time Out Live Award 2001 for Best New Play in the West End. Leo Butler won the George Devine Award 2001 for Most Promising Playwright for Redundant. Roy Williams won the Evening Standard's Charles Wintour Award 2001 for Most Promising Playwright for Clubland. Grae Cleugh won the 2001 Olivier Award for Most Promising Playwright for Fucking Games. Richard Bean was joint winner of the George Devine Award 2002 for Most Promising Playwright for Under the Whaleback. Caryl Churchill won the 2002 Evening Standard Award for Best New Play for A Number. Vassily Sigarev won the 2002 Evening Standard Charles Wintour Award for Most Promising Playwright for Plasticine. Ian MacNeil won the 2002 Evening Standard Award for Best Design for A Number and Plasticine. Peter Gill won the 2002 Critics' Circle Award for Best New Play for The York Realist (English Touring Theatre). Ché Walker won the 2003 George Devine Award for Most Promising Playwright for Flesh Wound. Lucy Prebble won the 2003 Critics' Circle Award and the 2004 George Devine Award for Most Promising Playwright, and the TMA Theatre Award 2004 for Best New Play for The Sugar Syndrome. Linda Bassett won the 2004 TMA Theatre Award for Best Actress (for Leo Butler's Lucky Dog). Laura Wade was joint winner of the George Devine Award 2005 for Breathing Corpses.

ROYAL COURT BOOKSHOP

The Royal Court bookshop offers a range of contemporary plays and publications on the theory and practice of modern drama. The staff specialise in assisting with the selection of audition monologues and scenes.
Many Royal Court playtexts from past and present productions cost £2.
The Bookshop is situated in the downstairs ROYAL COURT BAR AND FOOD.
Monday–Friday 3–10pm, Saturday 2.30–10pm
For information tel: 020 7565 5024
or email: bookshop@royalcourttheatre.com

PROGRAMME SUPPORTERS

The Royal Court (English Stage Company Ltd) receives its principal funding from Arts Council England, London. It is also supported financially by a wide range of private companies, charitable and public bodies, and earns the remainder of its income from the box office and its own trading activities.

The Genesis Foundation supports International Playwrights and the Young Writers' Festival. The Jerwood Charity supports new plays by new playwrights through the Jerwood New Playwrights series.

The Skirball Foundation funds a Playwrights' Programme at the theatre. The Artistic Director's Chair is supported by a lead grant from The Peter Jay Sharp Foundation, contributing to the activities of the Artistic Director's office. Bloomberg Mondays, the Royal Court's reduced price ticket scheme, is supported by Bloomberg. Over the past eight years the BBC has supported the Gerald Chapman Fund for directors.

MARTIN CRIMP

Fewer Emergencies

Whole Blue Sky
Face to the Wall
Fewer Emergencies

faber and faber

First published in this collection in 2005
by Faber and Faber Limited
3 Queen Square, London WC1N 3AU

Typeset by Country Setting, Kingsdown, Kent CT14 8ES
Printed in England by Mackays of Chatham plc, Chatham, Kent

A CIP record for this book
is available from the British Library

ISBN 0-571-23082-2

2 4 6 8 10 9 7 5 3 1

WHOLE BLUE SKY

Three actors required
1 (female), 2 *and* 3

Time
Blank

Place
Blank

/ *indicates point of overlap in overlapping dialogue*

2   She gets married very young, doesn't she.

3   Does what?

2   Gets married, gets married very young, and
     immediately realises——

3   Oh? That it's a mistake?

2   Immediately realises——yes——that it's a mistake.

3   She doesn't love him.

2   Oh yes, she loves him, she definitely loves him, but
     it's a mistake all the same.

3   Loving him makes it worse.

2   Makes it far far worse. Loving him makes it far far
     worse. What can she say? She can't say 'I don't love
     you'——it wouldn't be true. And at the same time
     what does she see?

3   Her whole life?

2   She sees——that's right——her whole life stretched
     out in front of her like a . . . hmm . . .

3   Corpse?

1   Corpse?——no——no——what?——no——that's
     not the way she thinks——it's more like a motorway
     at night——a band of concrete stretched out in front
     of her with reflective signs counting off the miles——
     mile after mile after mile.

Pause.

She's not sure what to do.

3   Oh?

1   No——not at all sure what to do.

2   Leave him.

1   Well of course——yes——leave him——talk to him very tenderly next to——well for example the river——talk to him next to the river just where the water swirls round the piers of the stone bridge. Talk to him: patiently explain that she's made a mistake——she loves him, but she's made a mistake.

2   She'll touch his cheek.

1   That's right: touch his cheek, ask him not to cry, explain it's for the best, touch his cheek, take his hand, comfort him——

3   As best she can.

1   Comfort him——obviously as best she can—— then get away. Pack and leave. Pick out just the few books she really values, because what else does she want?——all she wants is those few books and to be free——pack the books and leave.

2   So she packs the books and leaves.

1   I'm sorry?

2   Packs the books.

3   Packs the books and leaves.

1   Ha.

3   What's funny?

1   Packs the books and leaves? No.

2   She gets pregnant.

1   She packs nothing. She says nothing. Not by the river, not in fact anywhere. She gets——and that's exactly what happens——gets pregnant——gets pregnant very young and has the baby. Look: there it is.

2   There it is screaming.

3   She can't love it.

1   Can't what?

3   Love it——can't love the baby——gets depressed.

1   Gets what?

3   Depressed——gets depressed——depressed by all that screaming——all that sucking——all that biting the breast.

1   Oh no. She loves it. She loves the child. She loves the way it sucks——even the way it bites. Loves its hair, loves its eyes.

2   Loving it makes it worse.

3   Oh? Makes what worse? The marriage?

2   Loving the baby makes the marriage worse.

1   Loving the baby *cements* the marriage.

2   Does what?

3   Cements it.

1   It cements the marriage. Yes. Oh yes. The three of them make a picture.

2   What kind of picture?

1   A picture of happiness.

2   What kind of picture of happiness?

1   What d'you mean: what kind of picture of happiness?

2   What does a picture of happiness look like?

1   It looks like them.

3   Oh?

1   It looks like the three of them——yes——in their winter hats. It looks like the three of them in the pet shop selecting a pet. It looks just how they look in the toy shop selecting a toy: pictures, pictures of happiness: that's what a picture of happiness looks like.

2   So she doesn't know.

1   Doesn't know what? What is there to know? She knows what the good schools are, she knows what TV programmes are or are not acceptable, she knows the importance of fruit, she knows what time of day the blackbird visits the garden and when the blackbird visits the garden she says 'Oh look: there's the blackbird visiting the garden.'

2   So she doesn't know.

1   Of course she knows——doesn't know what?

2   About the things he gets up to.

3   Oh? Does he get up to things?

2   Of course he gets / up to things.

1   Of course she knows——of course he gets up to things——she's not stupid——she knows what it means when his eyes slide away like that.

3 Oh? Under the winter hat?

1 She knows he gets up to things——yes, under the hat——even in the toy shop selecting a toy his eyes still slide away. She knows what's on his mind.

2 So she packs her books, takes the child and leaves.

1 Does what?

2 Packs her books——takes her child——leaves.

1 What books?

Pause.

What books?

2 The books.

3 The books she had at the beginning.

1 Did she have books at the beginning then?

3 Of course she had books at the beginning: student books.

1 (*smiles*) Oh *those*: student books.

3 That's right: the books she had at the beginning: student books.

1 (*smiles*) *Those* books——the difficult ones——the ones she had at the beginning——the ones she wrote her name in at the beginning——the books that made her feel alive at the beginning.

3 Yes: where are they now?

2 Good question.

3 What happened to those books?

2 Good question.

1   What happened to the books? Well the books are probably . . . hmm . . . somewhere in a plastic bag.

3   Oh?

1   Yes, in a . . . hmm in a plastic bag or something. Why?

2   So the books aren't part of the picture.

1   What picture?

2   The picture we were talking about: the picture of happiness.

1   (*smiles*) Oh *that*: the picture of happiness. You mean the picture of the boat: the two of them on the boat.

3   The boat? No. Not two of them on the boat, three of them in the pet shop, three of them buying the pet. What boat?

Pause.

What boat?

1   (*inward*) Ha.

3   What's funny?

1   (*inward*) That pet——that pet's so funny——the way it knows the difference between right and wrong—— the way it burrows when it's done right and when it's done wrong comes to the surface——comes to the surface——smiles at everyone——shows us its yellow teeth. And the name's so funny. What a funny thing for a pet to call its own child. What kind of name is that?

2   You mean for a child to call its own pet.

1   I said for a child to call its own pet.

2   You said for a pet to call its own child.

1   You think I don't know what I said?

3   Well we won't argue.

1   We won't argue because what I said was to call its own pet——what a funny thing for a child to call its / own pet.

2   So you're saying she's still there?

1   Still where?

2   She hasn't left the house?

1   Left? No. Why? Because of the things he gets up to? Why? No. Why should she? Look at the floors. Look at the walls. Look at the way the dining table extends and extends. On summer evenings it extends and extends right through the French doors and out under the Blue Atlas Cedar. Small lamps hang in the branches and everybody's laughing: the doctors and nurses, the butchers and the musicians who have become their friends: work friends, boating friends, friends from school——parents——traders and craftspeople with exceptionally rare skills——the very same people in fact who designed and built then polished with their own hands this ever-lengthening table where everybody sits under the blue tree and laughs in a boisterous but good-natured way—— I stress good-natured way——about all those things that make life worth living. Of course she's still there.

3   Of course she is.

1   Leave? Why should she?

2   What things are those?

1   She has no intention, thank you very much, of leaving.

2   What things are those?

1   What things are what?

2   Money? Property? Family?——The things that make life worth living.

1   (*smiles*) Oh *those*. Say that again.

2   Money? Property? Family? What is it?

3   Yes, what is it that makes the guests laugh so good-naturedly?

1   Why shouldn't they laugh?

3   I'm sorry?

1   Why shouldn't her guests laugh? Why shouldn't her guests enjoy themselves under the tree? Haven't they worked? Haven't they struggled to extend this table? Haven't they screamed at each other in private? Punched each other? Haven't they broken each other's skin to open this, for example, bottle of wine?

3   Oh?

2   Of course they have.

1   Of course they have.

2   Used the word bitch.

1   Used the word pig. Used the phrase——hmm . . . what's that phrase?

3   'Say that one more fucking time and I'll break your fucking neck'?

1   Used the phrase——exactly——'say that one more fucking time to me and I'll break your fucking neck' in order to hang the tree, for example, with these tiny lamps.

2   You mean they have a right to laugh.

1   More than a right: they have a duty——just as when they toast each other they have a duty to meet each other's eyes.

3   I thought his eyes always slide away.

2   Not any more.

1   That's right: not any more. Now they stare back. After these——hmm . . . what is it? . . .

She silently counts, using her fingers.

. . . eleven——after these eleven years of marriage his grey eyes stare right back at hers.

2   Just as her grey eyes –

1   Exactly.

2   – stare right back –

1   Exactly——how did you know that?——into his.

3   'What is it you want, sweetheart?'

1 silently counts again on her fingers.

1   (*inward*) Or is it ten?

3   'What is it you want, sweetheart?'

1   (*looks up from counting*) What's that? I'm sorry?

2   She's asking him what he wants.

1   Asking who?

2   Asking Bobby.

1   Which Bobby?

3   Bobby her child.

1   (*smiles*) Oh *Bobby*——*that* Bobby——Bobby her
     child. Why? What does he want? Can't he sleep?
     What's wrong with him?

2   Maybe he'd like some fruit.

1   Maybe he'd like, yes, one of these plums. Or maybe
     he'd like just the tiniest sip of wine? No? What's that
     he's saying?

3   He's saying he can hear a noise.

1   What noise? That's just the guests laughing about all
     the things that make life worth living.

3   He's saying it's not the guests.

1   Not the guests? Then I'll tell you who it is: it must
     be Bobby.

3   He's saying no not Bobby.

1   Because Bobby is nocturnal. You know what
     nocturnal means. Nocturnal means that when you,
     Bobby, are asleep, that's when he——Bobby——
     starts tunnelling.

3   He's saying no not Bobby.

1   Because what did we say to you?——we said to you:
     don't keep Bobby in your room——Bobby is very
     nice but Bobby is nocturnal——which means that
     when you, Bobby, are asleep, he——the Bobby
     you have insisted and insisted on keeping in your
     room——starts cleaning out his nest.

2   He's saying no not Bobby: it's a voice.

3   A voice? In the room?

2   In his head: he's saying it's a voice in his head.

1   (*smiles*) Well we all have those, sweetheart, we all
    have voices in our heads: those are our thoughts.
    That's when Mummy talks to Mummy: that's when
    Mummy says 'Where did I leave my hair-clips,
    Mummy?' and Mummy answers 'Well Mummy, I'm
    not sure: have you tried looking in the bathroom?'
    Or Mummy might say to Mummy 'Why when I
    smile does it always feel like I'm smiling in spite of
    myself? Why have I stopped feeling alive, Mummy,
    the way I used to feel alive at the beginning?' Or
    'Why——Mummy——has my hair begun to turn
    the colour of cigarette-ash?' So Mummy has to get
    quite tough with Mummy then. Mummy has to
    say things to Mummy like 'Pull yourself together,
    Mummy, and grow up' or things like 'Ten or eleven
    years of marriage don't make a woman any less
    desirable——'

3   Far from it.

1   Far from it——yes——'Any more than do a few
    flecks of grey.' These are our thoughts.

2   He's saying no not thoughts. He knows what
    thoughts are, but this is a voice. He says the voice
    doesn't like him. He wants you to come.

1   Of course the voice likes him. What does he mean?

2   He wants you to come. He wants you to sit with
    him.

1   Of course the voice likes him. Everybody likes him.
    What is it exactly this voice is saying, sweetheart?

3   Good question.

1 Well?

Pause.

   Well?

2 He's saying the voice is too soft to make out.

1 Then how does he know it doesn't like him?

3 Good question.

1 Everybody likes him. Everybody has always liked him. Mummy——Daddy——people in shops—— people in the street——people on market stalls have always offered Jimmy, for example a banana——bent down, hooked cherries / over his ears.

2 Offered Bobby.

1 What?

2 Have always offered Bobby, for example a banana ——bent down, hooked cherries / over his ears.

1 I said Bobby.

3 You said Jimmy.

1 Well whatever I said AND I KNOW FOR A FACT I SAID BOBBY people have always liked him: always offered him fruit, always offered him love, pulled down his winter hat to keep his / head snug.

2 He wants you to sit with him. He wants you / to sing.

1 Bought him pets, built him snowmen, assembled his jigsaws late at night so that in the morning he'd come down the spiral stairs to find the sky, and I mean the whole blue sky completed, cut the crusts off his sandwiches and taken / the cheese out.

2   He wants you to sing the / little song.

1   Clipped his fingernails——wants me to what?

2   To sing.

3   To sing the little song.

    Pause.

1   (*cold*) Oh?

3   Yes.

1   Wants me to sing the little song.

3   Yes.

1   What does he mean?

2   Good question.

3   To blot out?

1   I'm sorry?

3   Is it to blot out?

2   Yes——good answer: maybe to blot out the voice?

1   What voice?

3   (*mocks*) 'What voice?'

1   (*smiles*) Oh *that*——the *voice*——well yes it may well be to 'blot out the voice' but listen——

3   Oh?

1   That song, the little song, that's . . . well . . . hmm . . . that's Mummy and Daddy's song.

3   Oh?

1   That is——yes, that is a private song.

3 Oh?

1 And don't keep saying oh like that because it is as you very well know a private song.

3 Oh?

2 A private song?

1 Yes it is Mummy and Daddy's private song and I don't want to hear you talk about it ever again.

3 Not ever again?

1 That's right.

2 Says who?

3 Says who? Says Mummy.

1 Is that understood: I don't want to hear you talk about it ever again.

2 In front of guests.

1 In front of guests. In front of anyone. Not tonight and not ever again.

2 Says who?

1 I'm sorry?

2 Says who: not tonight and not ever again.

3 Says who? Says Mummy.

1 Says what?

3 Says Mummy.

1 (*smiles*) Not says Mummy, sweetheart, not says Mummy: says the voice.

FACE TO THE WALL

Four actors required
1 (male), 2, 3 *and* 4

Time
Blank

Place
Blank

/ *indicates point of overlap in overlapping dialogue*

1   Yes? says the receptionist, What can I do for you? How can I help you? Who did you want to see? Do you have an appointment?

2   He shoots her through the mouth.

1   He shoots her through the mouth and he goes down the corridor.

3   Quite quickly.

1   Goes——good——yes——quite quickly down the corridor——opens the first door he finds.

3   Walks straight in.

1   Walks straight in.

2   Yes? says the teacher, How can I help you?

1   Shoots him through the heart.

3   Shoots the teacher right through the heart.

1   The children don't understand——they don't immediately grasp what's going on——what's happened to their teacher?——they don't understand——nothing like this has ever / happened before.

3   Nothing like this has ever happened before——but they do understand——of course they understand—— they've seen this on TV——they've stayed up late as a special treat and they've seen this on TV——they know exactly what's going on and this is why they back away——instinctively back away.

1   Okay——so they back away——the worst thing they could do——back away——but they back away—— they back away against the wall.

2   Against their pictures on the wall——'My house'.

3   'My cat'.

2   'Me and my cat'.

3   'My house', 'Me and my cat', 'Me in a tree', and it's interesting to see the way that some of them / hold hands.

1   And it's interesting to see the way that some of them hold hands——they instinctively hold hands——the way children do——the way a child does——if you reach for its hand as it walks next to you it will grasp your own——not like an adult who will flinch away——never touch an adult's hand like this or the adult will flinch away——unless it's someone who loves you——a loved one——anyone else will flinch away——but a loved one will take your hand like a child——they will trust you like a child——a loved one won't flinch away——a loved one will hold your hand because the hand reminds you of your love—— whole afternoons for example spent simply feeling the spaces between each other's fingers——or looking into the loved one's eyes——the thick rings of colour in the loved one's eyes——which are like something——what is it?——don't help me——the precipitate——the precipitate in a test tube——but anyone else——an adult——will flinch away——just as the child——child A——now flinches away from what?——yes?

4   From the warm metal.

1   From the warm metal——thank you——of the gun.

Just as child A now flinches away from the warm metal of the gun. He shoots child A——in the head.

3 He moves on.

1 He moves on to child B. He shoots child B——in the head.

3 He moves on.

1 He moves on to child C. Child C——yes?

4 Tries to duck away.

1 What?

4 Child C tries / to duck away.

1 He shoots child B——in the head.

3 He moves on.

1 He moves on to child C. Child C tries to duck away. He shoots——no——yes——no——not shoots——yes?

4 But to no avail.

1 Tries to duck away. But to no avail. He shoots child A——in the head.

3 He moves on.

1 He moves on to child B. He shoots child B——in the head.

3 He moves on.

1 He moves on to child C. Child C tries to duck away. But to no avail. But to no avail. He shoots child C——good——in the head.

2 And how's life treating him?

1 What?

2   Life——how's life treating him?

1   Life's treating him very well.

3   How's his job?

1   His job is fine——well paid and rewarding.

3   And his wife?

1   Is charming and tolerant.

2   And how are his children?

1   His children are fine.

3   How many does he have now?

1   Four. He has four and all four of them are fine.

2   What? All four of them are fine?

1   All four——yes——is this right?——are absolutely fine. He loves swinging them through the air and hearing them scream with joy. When he gets back to their beautiful house he picks them off the ground and swings them screaming through the air.

3   And how is his beautiful house?

1   Increasing in value daily——well constructed and well located——close to amenities——schools—— shops——major roads leading directly to major airports——minor roads——no——yes——minor roads——yes——minor roads winding——is it?—— don't help me——don't help me——yes——minor roads winding through meadows watered by springs welling up through the chalk.

3   And how are the schools in his neighbourhood?

1   The schools in his neighbourhood are fine.

3   And the shops?

2   Yes——how's the shopping?

1   Excellent shopping——excellent——yes?

4   And not just the big names.

1   And not just the big names. Excellent shopping——
excellent——and not just the big names but——yes?

4   Those kinds of / smaller shops.

1   Excellent shopping——excellent——and not just the
big names but those kinds of smaller shops you
thought——not thought——imagined?——yes?

4   You thought had all but / disappeared.

1   Disappeared. Excellent shopping——excellent——
and not just the big names but those kinds of smaller
shops you thought had all but disappeared.

3   I thought those smaller shops had all but
disappeared.

1   Well yes they have——but not here——not here——
here you can find all those kinds of smaller shops
you thought had all but disappeared. *He moves on.*

2   What? Artisans?

1   Artisans——yes——people who bind books——
people who make shoes——people who grind
knives——people who mend rugs——people who
gut fish——cut cheese——people who mix paint.
He moves on.

3   Medical supplies?

1   Medical supplies——catering supplies——motoring
supplies——yes?

4   Spare parts / for cars.

1   Spare parts for cars no longer manufactured but lovingly restored. He moves on. He shoots child D——in the head.

2   So there must be blood.

1   Well of course there's blood——not just blood on the wall——not just blood on the floor.

3   But blood in the air.

2   Blood in the air. Blood hanging in the air. A mist.

3   An aerosol.

1   An aerosol——that's right——that's good——of blood——which he hadn't foreseen——he hadn't foreseen the aerosol of blood——or the sound——is this right?——this is right——or the sound of the distressed children when his head was on the white pillow——on the white pillow——don't help me—— when his head was on the white pillow picturing the scene——but now——don't help me——but now it's clear——now the picture is clear——and there's another sound——what's that other sound?—— don't help me, don't help me——the sound of his heart——no——yes——yes——the sound of his heart——the sound of his own heart——the sound of the killer's heart sounding in the killer's head—— that's right——that's good——which he hadn't foreseen——he hadn't foreseen the sound of his own heart in his own head——filling his head—— his own heart filling his head with blood——popping his ears——popping his ears with blood——like a swimmer——not swimmer——don't help me—— like a diver——this is right——diving into blood—— he's like a diver diving into blood——that's right——that's good——very good——down he goes——down he goes away from the light——

diving into blood——popping——popping his ears
and what are you staring at?——eh?——eh?——
what are you staring at?——turn away——look
away——no——turn away——that's right——turn
away or you're next——be quiet or you're next——
that's right——that's good——you saw what
happened to child A, you saw what happened to
child B, you saw what happened to child C——you
saw what happened to child C——you saw what
happened to child C——no——yes——no——don't
help me——

Pause.

Don't help me——

4   You saw what happened to child D.

1   Don't help me——you saw what happened to child
A, you saw what happened to child B, you saw what
happened to child C, you saw what happened to
child D, so——so——you saw what happened to
child D, so——

4   So shut the / fuck up.

1   YOU SAW WHAT HAPPENED TO CHILD D, SO SHUT
THE FUCK UP. CUNT. CUNT. LITTLE CUNT. I SAID
DON'T HELP ME.

Long pause.

3   So he's not a sympathetic character.

1   No.

3   We can't feel for him.

1   No.

3   Cry for him.

1   No.

3   He's never suffered.

1   No.

3   Experienced war.

1   No.

3   Experienced poverty.

1   No.

2   Torture.

1   Torture?

2   Been tortured——yes——for his beliefs. You heard
     what / I said.

1   No. What beliefs? No.

2   Abused, then, as a child.

1   No.

2   Fucked up the arse as a child.

1   No.

3   Or in the mouth.

1   No.

2   Beaten.

3   Beaten by his dad breaking a leg off the chair in the
     kitchen. Beaten with a chair-leg.

1   No.

2   What about his own children?

3   Yes——perhaps they're sick.

1   No.

2   His wife?

3   His wife what?

2   Sick?

1   No.

2   Is his car unreliable?

1   No.

2   What about the milkman?

3   Yes——is the milkman in his neighbourhood ever late?

1   No.

2   Or the postman?

1   Sometimes.

Pause.

3   How does he feel when the postman's late?

1   Angry.

2   So now he's going to kill the postman.

3   Typical.

1   Of course he's not going to kill the postman. It's not the postman's fault——he knows it's not the postman's fault——sometimes there are problems sorting the letters——the machine for sorting the letters has broken down, for example, and the letters have to be sorted by hand——or perhaps there are lots of parcels and every parcel means a conversation on the doorstep.

Pause.

A conversation on the doorstep——yes?

33

4   In the sunshine.

1   Means a conversation on the doorstep in the
    sunshine. And sometimes the postman's boy can't
    wake the postman up. 'Dad, dad', he says 'it's five
    o'clock'——

4   'Wake up. It's five o'clock.'

1   'Dad, dad,' he says, 'Wake up. It's five o'clock. I've
    brought you / your tea.'

4   'Time to get up.'

1   What?

4   'Time / to get up.'

1   'Dad, dad,' he says, 'Wake up. It's five o'clock. Time
    to get up. I've brought you your tea.' But the
    postman——don't help me——but the postman——
    this is right——I'm right——don't help me——'Time
    to get up. I've brought you your tea.' But the
    postman——but the postman——but the postman
    just pushes himself harder against the wall.

*

Twelve-Bar Delivery Blues

Woke up this morning
Heard my son call
Turned away from the window
Turned my face to the wall.
Daddy daddy, he said to me
Daddy daddy, I've BROUGHT YOU YOUR TEA.

FACE TO THE WALL

Son, I told him,
Your poor daddy's dead
There's another person
Come to live in his head.
Son son, your daddy's not well
Son son, your DADDY'S A SHELL.

There's another person
Speaking these lies
There's another person
Looking out through my eyes.
Son son, he's filing reports
Son son, he's PROMPTING MY THOUGHTS.

My son poured tea
From the brown china pot
Said, drink up your tea, dad,
Drink up while it's hot.
Daddy daddy, you're not sick at all
Daddy daddy, turn a-WAY FROM THE WALL.

Hey daddy,
You're a liar——and a fake
Take off those pyjamas
There's deliveries to make.
I lifted my head from my white pillow case
Threw my hot tea RIGHT IN HIS FACE.

Hey sonny,
If there's one thing I've learned
It's don't rub on butter
When your skin is all burned.
Son son, I ain't got no choice
Son son, I JUST HEAR THIS VOICE
(Saying . . .)

Doo ba ba-doo ba ba – Doo ba ba-doo ba ba –
Doo ba ba-doo ba ba – Doo ba ba-doo ba ba –
Doo ba ba-doo ba ba – Doo ba ba-doo ba ba –
Doo ba ba-doo ba ba – Doo ba ba-doo ba ba –
Doo ba ba-doo ba ba – Doo ba ba-doo ba ba –
Doo ba ba-doo ba ba – DOO DOO DOO DOO . . .

Woke up this morning
Heard my son call
Turned away from the window
Turned my face to the wall.
Son son, I hear what you say
But there just ain't gonna be no deliveries today . . .
(No way).

FEWER EMERGENCIES

Three actors required
1, 2 *and* 3

Time
Blank

Place
Blank

/ indicates point of overlap in overlapping dialogue

2 And how are things going?

1 Well things are improving. Things are improving day by day.

2 What kind of things?

1 Well, the light. The light is improving day by day.

2 Getting brighter?

1 What?

2 Getting brighter? Getting brighter day by day? Improving day by day? Getting brighter?

1 What?

2 Getting brighter? Getting brighter day by day? Improving.

1 Oh yes. Yes. Improving, yes. Getting brighter, yes.

2 Good.

1 Getting so much brighter, yes.

2 Good. I'm pleased.

1 I'm happy you're pleased.

2 I'm pleased about the light.

1 I'm pleased about the light too.

3 We're all pleased about the light.

2 Well, yes, of course we are——and are they still boating?

41

1   Both of them are still boating.

3   What? Gliding past?

1   Both of them are still gliding past when they get the chance, and they get the chance more and more often. More and more often they get the boat out——they set sail——they glide past in the boat.

3   So things are improving.

1   They're improving day by day. Not just the light, but boating too. They get the boat out——they check the supplies——they test the satellite telephone——they leave the estuary——and before you know it they're out on the ocean——slicing through the waves—— travelling further and further afield.

3   More confidently.

1   Much more confidently.

2   How do they look?

1   Look?

3   Yes——good question——how do they look?

1   Well, confident——more confident.

3   You mean they're smiling? Or don't they need to smile?

2   They don't need to smile but they're smiling anyway.

3   What——in spite of themselves?

1   They're smiling——that's right——in spite of themselves. Or rather——no——correction——they know they're smiling——but equally they know the kind of smile they're smiling resembles the kind of smile you smile in spite of yourself.

3 Say that again.

1 I can't say that again, but what I can say is that they still sing that little song.

2 They don't.

1 They do.

2 They don't.

1 They do, they do, they still sing that little song like something you hear in the supermarket.

3 Or in the DIY superstore, or on the porno film——when the swollen cock on the porno film goes into the swollen cunt.

2 So things are looking up.

1 Things are definitely looking up——brighter light——more frequent boating——more confident smile——things are improving day by day——who ever would've guessed?

2 Mmm?

1 Who ever would've guessed? Who ever would've thought the two of them could set sail like that towards the world's rim?

3 World's what?

1 World's rim. The rim of the world. The edge.

2 What edge? There is no edge of the world.

1 Oh yes there is. Oh yes there is an edge of the world.

2 Well, we won't argue.

1 We won't argue because there is an edge of the world——it's as simple as that. There's a rim like the rim of a plate, and past the rim is——what?

43

3   We don't know.

1   We don't know——it's as simple as that——we don't know what's past the / rim of the world.

2   So how are things looking when they leave the house?

1   Things are looking great. Things are improving. The whole neighbourhood is improving. The trees are more established, they've kicked out the Mexicans, they've kicked out the Serbs, people are finally cleaning up their own dog-mess, nice families are moving in.

2   Italians and Greeks?

3   Greeks, Italians, nice Chinese.

1   Nice Somalis, nice Chinese, really nice Kurds, really nice families who clean up their own dog-mess and hoover the insides of their cars. And what's more they've identified the gene——no——correction—— they've identified the sequence——that's right—— of genes that make people leave burnt mattresses outside their homes and strangled their babies.

2   Oh?

1   Yes——strangled their babies and installed better street lighting. Things are looking up. It's taken time of course. They've aged. Their hair's gone grey. But it doesn't stop them being desirable——far from it.

3   It doesn't stop them being desirable——it doesn't stop them boating——it doesn't stop them heading, like now, for the rim of the world——far from it—— or installing cupboards——

2   Far from it.

1   Far from it. It doesn't stop them installing cupboards for Bobby at the top of the spiral stairs——

3   Cupboards of precious wood.

1   Cupboards——that's right——of precious wood installed by joiners for all of Bobby's things——all the things Bobby will need in life for pleasure and for emergencies.

2   Candles?

1   Well naturally there are candles, boxes of matches, fresh figs, generators and barrels of oil. But there's also a shelf full of oak trees, and another where pine forests border a mountain lake. If you press a concealed knob a secret drawer pops open——inside is the island of Manhattan. And if you pull the drawers out, spilling the bone-handled knives and chickens onto the floor, spilling out the chain-saws and the harpsichords, there at the back, in the dark space at the back, is the city of Paris with a cloth over it to keep the dust out. There's a wardrobe full of uranium and another full of cobalt. Bobby's suits are hanging over a Japanese golf course. His shoes share boxes with cooked prawns. On one little shelf there's a row of universities——good ones—— separated by restaurants where chefs are using the deep-fryers to melt gold and cast it into souvenir life-sized Parthenons. And hanging from the shelf, like the Beethoven quartets and fertility clinics, is the key, the key to use in emergencies, the key to get out of the house.

3   You mean he's locked in?

1   Well of course Jimmy's locked in——he's always locked in——he's locked in for his own protection.

2 Bobby.

1 What?

2 Bobby——not Jimmy——Bobby is locked in for his own protection.

1 I said Bobby.

2 You said Jimmy.

1 You think I don't know what I said?

2 Well we won't argue.

1 We won't argue because what I said was / Bobby.

3 What emergencies?

1 Oh, didn't I tell you?

3 What emergencies?

1 Oh, didn't I tell you? Because there's an emergency on right now. Rocks are being thrown——shots fired——that kind of stuff.

3 What? Cars are being overturned?

1 Cars are being——exactly——overturned and burnt.

2 Surely not Bobby's car?

1 Of course not Bobby's car——Bobby's not old enough to drive——but Bobby's neighbours' cars, Bobby's friends' cars, Bobby's parents' cars——yes——of course——are being first turned on their sides, then completely overturned, and burnt.

2 I thought things were improving.

1 Things *are* improving——less rocks are thrown—— less cars completely overturned——less shots fired—— there are fewer emergencies than there used to be—— but all the same, there's an emergency on right now.

46

It's on right now. And I'm sorry to say that one of those shots came through the kitchen window and caught poor Bobby in the hip.

2   Oh?

1   Yes——I'm afraid so——it caught poor Bobby in the hip which is why instead of running up those stairs, he's——what?

3   He's crawling?

1   He's crawling——that's right——that's good——up the spiral stairs. Using his arms mainly.

2   He wants to reach the key.

1   He wants to open the door.

2   He must be mad.

3   Open the door? He must be / completely mad.

1   Ah yes——but you have to know what's going on in Bobby's mind. In Bobby's mind, if he opens the door, if he lets people in, if he takes them up the stairs, shows them the cupboards of precious wood, the fresh figs, the knives and the uranium——if he lifts a corner of the cloth and gives them a glimpse of Paris——if he shows them the swollen cock going into the swollen cunt and lets them pick a restaurant or a string quartet——if, after a swim in the mountain lake, he lets them take home a human egg——then what?——they'll what?——they'll . . . Yes?

3   Love him.

2   They'll love him

1   Then they'll always love him.

     Pause.

     Exactly.

3   Ship to shore.

1   What?

3   Ship to shore. They're calling him from the boat.
    They're calling him from the rim of the world on the
    satellite telephone. 'Bobby? Are you there?'

2   He's not answering.

1   Well of course he's not answering. He's pulling
    himself up the spiral stairs. He wants to get / to the
    key.

3   'Pick up the phone, Bobby.'

1   He's got the hang of it now: pull with the arms——
    let the legs drag——concentrate.

2   So things are looking up.

3   Things are definitely looking up——more efficient
    use of his arms——more understanding of the
    geometry of the stairs——improved / concentration.

1   Brighter light——more frequent boating——more
    confident smile——fewer / emergencies.

2   It doesn't worry them then?

1   What?

2   It doesn't worry them that Bobby's not answering.

1   Of course it worries them——that's why they
    smile——that's why they sing that little song.

2   They don't.

1   They do.

2   They don't.

1   They do, they do——they push their grey hair out of
    their bright grey eyes and sing that little song.

3   (*sings – very soft and relaxed scat-singing*)
    Doo doo-ba-dee doo doo doo ba-doo . . .
    Ba doo-ba-dee doo, ba doo-ba dee doo . . .

    *Say ten seconds of this. Then slight pause. Then the
    others join in unison, singing longer and more
    intense phrases. The lights begin a slow fade,
    reaching black where indicated.*

1, 2, 3
    Doo doo-ba-dee doo doo doo ba-doo . . .
    Ba doo-ba-dee doo, ba doo-ba dee doo . . .
    Ba doo-ba doo doo doo-ba doo-ba dee doo . . .

    *Maybe twenty-five seconds of this. Then pause.
    Lights still fading.*

3   And Bobby?

1   Mmm?

3   And Bobby?

1   What he's losing in blood he's gaining in confidence.
    Light's flaring through the windows——flames——
    it's getting brighter——he can see the key——

    Black.

2   Things are improving.

1   Things are improving. He's further up the stairs. He's
    closer to the key. See how it spins——no——
    correction——swings——see how / it swings.

2   See how the key swings.

3   That's right, Bobby-boy. Watch the key. Watch the
    key swinging.